Dead Opposite

Dead Opposite

The Lives and Loss of
Two American Boys

**GEOFFREY
DOUGLAS**

Henry Holt and Company   New York

Henry Holt and Company, Inc.
Publishers since 1866
115 West 18th Street
New York, New York 10011

Henry Holt® is a registered
trademark of Henry Holt and Company, Inc.

Library of Congress Cataloging-in-Publication Data
Douglas, Geoffrey.
   Dead opposite: the lives and loss of two American
boys/ Geoffrey Douglas. — 1st ed.
      p.   cm.
   1. Murder—Connecticut—New Haven.   2. Prince,
Christian Haley, 1971–1991.   3. Fleming, James
Duncan.   4. United States—Social conditions—
1980–   .   I. Title.
HV6534.N4D68   1995
364.1'523'097468—dc20   94-9615
                                                           CIP

                    ISBN 0-8050-2686-X

Henry Holt books are available for special promotions
and premiums. For details contact:
Director, Special Markets.

First Edition—1995

Designed by Paula R. Szafranski

Printed in the United States of America
All first editions are printed on acid-free paper.∞

            1   3   5   7   9   10   8   6   4   2

To my son, Sam,
still too young to know his own preciousness,
with a prayer that our world will grow kinder
before he is old enough to learn . . .

Author's Note

This story, while inspired by a murder, is not a true-crime tale. I have little taste for those. And, although driven by the schisms that divide race and class, it is not a social tract. I am neither sociologist nor scholar, and would not pretend to be.

What I do best as a writer (it may be *all* I do truly well, though I prefer to think of this less as failing than strength) is to make people real. The realness of two families is the force behind this book.

One is white and more than comfortable, the other black and poor. Their lives intersected—perhaps on a New Haven street on a February 1991 night, when a teenage boy died randomly; certainly in a courtroom many months later, when both families, each in its way, were on trial.

Real people, no matter the skill of those who portray them, are lost in translation unless, in the end, they translate themselves. These people have. Both families, the Princes and the Flemings, have shared more honesty with me in their living rooms than some of the best friends I've had. Shame, sorrow, pride, rage, frustration, impotence, loss—they have aired it all, as shamelessly as I could have dared to hope. I could not be more grateful. It is to their trust and nakedness that I owe this book.

And so: to Duncan Fleming, the only principal now alive, who allowed me into his world when there was nothing to gain in doing so; to Ted and Sally, Jim and Julia, Jackie, Teddy, Tanya, and Sandra—all of whose loss has been too great for words, but who found the words, anyway, to share it;

And to one other: Christian Prince, the second principal, whose gravestone, letters, and pictures had to speak for him, but who spoke as loudly as anyone alive.

Thank you, all of you. I am indebted.

And to the others, without whom this portrait would have had only two sides: Joe LaMotta, Mike Dearington, Frank Iannotti, Susan Storey, Ellen Knight, Tim Shriver, Scott X, "Merlin," Roger Vann, Larry Downs, Jim Adams, Diana Montgomery, Katrina Berger, Lawrence Deas—there is not one of you who did not add a color or a shade.

And thanks, too, to those at the New Haven Public Library; to Dave Leonhardt, then of the *Yale Daily News;* to *The New Yorker*'s William Finnegan, Peter Canellos of *The Boston Globe*, Jon Nordheimer of *The New York Times*, Joe Brady and Josh Kovner of the *New Haven Register,* and author Andrew Billingsley, all of whose works guided and informed my own.

Because this book portrays (with one exception) now-living people, whose circumstances changed—sometimes markedly —over the nearly two years it took to prepare and write, you will come upon some variances here: a "rolling" present tense, a boy of nineteen suddenly twenty, four children in a family you first met with only three.

You will, I hope, forgive these things. They are small and were inevitable—the product of lives being lived.

One final, critical note: I have attempted no dispassion here. From the strict perspectives of the journalist's trade, I have broken the cardinal rule. My feelings are in full view.

It was more than intentional; it was planned. I would have approached this story no other way. It is a story that depicts two worlds, as alien from one another as Jupiter from Earth; I am a member of one of them—I am white and grew up privileged—a stranger to the other. To have invited you to believe otherwise, through the artifice of a reporter's "distance," would have been to have created a lie. Or at least a smug fiction.

But there is a second, more useful reason for the presence of my voice. I am a parent, as are many of you. This story, in its purest state, is about parents and sons. The task of its telling seemed to offer, more than most nonfiction accounts, the chance to be a filter: the father-reporter, the conduit for empathy, through whose eyes and heart you might come to feel, from a three-foot distance, in living rooms, coffee shops, and jail cells, the misery and inconsolability of loss—of being black and impotent, or white and consumed by rage.

To have remained "distant" and "objective," however traditional or correct, would have been to have missed this chance. I am more than glad I took it.

Dead Opposite

The inscription, in three deep-cut lines across the center of the headstone, is derived from a schoolmaster's tribute to a then-living boy:

CHRISTIAN HALEY PRINCE
JULY 8, 1971 TO FEBRUARY 17, 1991
SCHOLAR, ATHLETE, LEADER, FRIEND

The grave site, a flat, gray, granite marker backed by a single row of holly trees, is barely a speck in the vastness of Washington's Rock Creek Cemetery. One of only two in the small family plot, all but invisible except from above, it seems a fitting memorial to a life only barely defined.

Its visitors—mother, father, sister, brother, a friend or uncle now and then—come most often in groups, nearly always on "special days." Christmas, Easter, Thanksgiving, the dreaded July eighth birthdays. Seasonal family pilgrimages of joy-reversed.

They bring the only gifts they can: evergreens in winter, bouquets of wildflowers from the family garden in April and July. Through the autumn months of the football season, a triangular maroon-and-gold pennant—Washington Redskins—flutters on a stick a foot from the grave, the lightsome invention of a close family friend. The first year it was placed, the Redskins went on to win the Super Bowl, assuring a tradition. The next year, of course, they did not.

He is a well-remembered young man. Remembered best, by those who knew him best, for his plainness, his quiet-smiling privacy, his open wonder at worlds not his own—Cree Indians, Arkansas rednecks, the aurora borealis—until the real world killed him one late night when his back was turned to it, in what should have been among its safest spots. There is no lesson in his death but that the lessons of life are sometimes more mockery than truth.

The other boy. Prisoner #203345 in the Manson Youth Correctional Facility in Cheshire, Connecticut, for a crime he says he didn't commit. It's not hard to believe him, for the evidence is slim. Or to doubt him, either, because of the boy he is: poor, black, dull eyed, an accused car thief and killer. He grew up in the ghetto, joined a gang at thirteen, got high every chance he had. He saw his first killing at ten years old, had sex before he was twelve, walks with a limp from a bullet through both legs. His best friends are drug dealers; he may have been one himself.

He sees death as "business," guns as "tools," his days in the street as "family time." He figures, he says, that if he weren't in jail he'd likely be "somewhere else." He smiles thinly as he says this, cocks his thumb and forefinger, points them at his ear, and yanks.

His name is James Duncan Fleming; James to his parents, "Dunc" to most everyone else. He is nineteen years old, the same age as the boy—Christian Prince—he was said to have killed, who would be twenty-three today. He, like the dead boy, was the third child of three. Both were born on the eighth of the month; both worshiped their fathers, who worshiped them back.

Beyond these small links, it is hard to fathom that even the air they breathe is drawn from the same source.

I never knew Christian Prince, or knew about him. He was dead more than a year before I knew he'd lived. The *New York Times* story that introduced us—"Son of Privilege, Son of Pain," the lead story in the Metro section on a Sunday in June of 1992—told of a boy "almost too good to be true": star athlete, honor-roll scholar, school leader ("the kindest guy I ever knew," a roommate remembered), a fourth-generation Yale student whose "blond good looks and trim, 6-foot-2 athletic frame seemed to strain reality."

The dead boy's father, the story went on, "a prominent lawyer in Washington" and former doubles partner of George Bush, headed the family home in "the upper-middle class terraces of Chevy Chase, Md."

There was more. The story covered most of two pages, including photos, 120 column-inches in all. It told of how Christian Prince had met his death and of the boy who'd been charged in his killing: the then-sixteen-year-old black gang member from "the bleak side streets of New Haven," who, "despite his parents' hopes, had scant reason to believe he could look forward to any but a narrow band of choices in life."

Both boys were pictured. The accused killer—skinheaded, mustached, lean but well muscled, in dark pants and white T-shirt, looking older than his years—half sits, half leans on a desktop in the warden's office of the New Haven city jail. His photo tops the page, three columns wide by nearly five inches deep, with the story's full headline—"Son of Privilege, Son of Pain: Random Death at Yale's Gate"—in four uneven black lines against the white cinderblock of the prison-office wall. The sense you get is of menace.

And the other picture, the victim's. Less than a quarter the size, it is centered between two columns of type an inch or so below the photo of the accused: smiling and squinting into the glint of sunlight off new Vermont snow, windblown blond hair matting his forehead, broad shoulders, straight white teeth— handsome, wholesome, a milk ad made real. I would learn later that the photo was the family's favorite.

And under it, this caption: "The murder of Christian Prince, a Yale sophomore, has sharply illuminated the differences between the lives of the haves and have-nots."

Murder as illumination. A white boy's death as the price of understanding a black boy's rage. Paradigms as principles, ignorance dispelled by line drawings from a reporter's notebook.

Maybe. If it works. If the drawings are full enough, if the heart can somehow be engaged. We are, after all, most of us, more voyeurs than Samaritans. And there *is* value in looking through windows—if we don't mistake what we see for what it is not.

■ ■ ■

This is a story about life—*two* lives, and the lives that surround them—about death, waste, grief as dark as the darkest canyon of the deepest sea on earth, hope and hopelessness, courage, cowardice, dignity, love that nurtures and love too dulled to act, survival, injustice, economics, the skill and science we call the American Way.

And the utter, absolute futility of crafting perfect truth from any of it.

2

On a weekday evening in mid-July 1992, seventeen months after Ted and Sally Prince had lost their son, three weeks after I learned of his death in the *Times*, I arrived as a stranger to their home. I had come, this first time, more as salesman than writer: to enlist their blessing, and their help, in the telling of his story. Without them, we all three knew well, there could *be* no story.

The whole family was there: daughter Jackie, the firstborn, pretty and plainspoken, who would be thirty in three months, an engineer with the Environmental Defense Fund; and Ted Junior, five years younger, a second-year law student at Duke. Christian, their mother would tell me later that night, "was the baby. He would have been twenty-one this month."

It was a warm night, even for July in the Potomac Valley. We sat outside, the five of us, at a round, all-weather table on the patio by their swimming pool, sipping wine and talking, for most of the first hour, about Washington and its metroplex: inner-city gridlock, the spread of the suburbs, the troubles I'd had finding my way to their door.

It would be nearly dark before Christian's name was mentioned, close to midnight before the evening was done—and more than a month before they would give their final blessing to the story I wanted to tell. I was, for now, a stranger in their home, come to lift the lid on their grief at no price to myself. They were wary but gracious hosts.

We ate outdoors—"salad under the stars," someone called it —a meal that began when Ted Prince on one side, his daughter on the other, reached for my hand in the saying of grace: "Bless, O Lord, this food to our use and us to Thy service," it began. And ended: "Please take good care of Christian."

By degrees, over dinner, the strangeness lifted. We talked about their son, and mine: sixteen at the time, with many of the same privileges, hopes, and reasons to think well of life. I spoke of the spirit I would try to bring to the story, the importance I felt it had. All four asked questions; two of the four, at one time or another, cried. I asked almost no questions myself. It was a right I hadn't yet earned.

I had come prepared for their graciousness. For the comforts of their home and the affluence it spoke of, for the warmth I received and tried my best to return. This was a home of decent, privileged people. That much I'd known before I'd boarded the plane. It was much of why I'd come.

But there was more than that. There was a *purity* at the table that night. I could call it by no other name. A fractured family, openly in grief, sharing their tears with a stranger, without posturing or shyness, or wish of sympathy or gain. Our voices, all night, remained soft, almost muted. No one person, it seemed, counted for less or more: "Sally, I think, may not be comfortable with that," or, "I'm not sure Teddy feels the same." The troubles of one were the troubles of all.

The mother's anguish was easily the most visible, the brother's perhaps second. The sister was stoic, though wet eyed from time to time. The father took refuge in his pride—which glowed from him as though lit from within.

But what was remarkable for a family on display: There was no pandering to the more wounded ones, no hand-pats or knee-squeezes, or embarrassed, apologetic looks my way when a voice broke in midsentence or a face wrenched up in pain. If anything, it was the reverse: The smiles drew courage from the tears and grew wider; the tears passed, then went to smiles, then—sometimes—even to laughter. By the end of the night, there seemed little to tell between one and the next.

Their anger was as naked as their grief, though (for that night at least) nearly as muted. The death of her son, said Sally Prince—she'd said the same to the *Times*—"has made me question my belief in God." Christian's brother told of the gang members who'd been present at the trial a month before, of how they'd leered and taunted in the courtroom. The rage in his voice, and on his face, almost hurt to witness.

There would be less restraint in days to come, and some-times less to admire. But one thing, always, would be the same. As a family, they were a fortress. Violated, wounded, angry, often bitter, sometimes blinded in their grief—but re-newed and renewing, each by the other, in a strength that cannot be taught.

It was the way, I thought—and would think a hundred times as, over the months, I watched them grip their pain—that fam-ilies are *supposed* to work.

■ ■ ■

It was close to midnight. We had said our goodbyes and agreed to talk in a week. There was no certainty that we would meet again.

I was outside now, the door closed behind me, in the half-circle driveway in front of their home, rifling my pockets for the keys to a rental car. It was a still, clear night. There was barely a light on in the four or five homes I could see.

"Have you seen any pictures of Christian?" It was Ted Senior, looking sad and rumpled and a little abashed, alone in the doorway.

Only the one in the paper, I told him.

"C'mon back inside then," he said. "I'll show you some pictures."

It was more command than invitation. The look on his face was as flat as a ghost's.

We went back in together. The downstairs lights were out. No one else was in sight.

For twenty more minutes, in a small sitting room to the left of the front hallway, Ted Prince showed me pictures: Christian in Vermont three weeks before his death (the same one I'd seen in the *Times*, but framed now and in color), as a Yale lacrosse player, a schoolboy defensive end, a dripping-wet teenager in a red bathing suit, a bleached-blond six-year-old with melting vanilla cone.

For each one, there was a story. Most, if not all, I would hear again. "I was there the game this was taken—I used to go to all his games. . . . This one, too. . . . This one here, I think, we were on vacation. . . . This was when he came back from out west, the summer before he died."

But there was no joy in the telling. Even the pride seemed gone. Ted Prince stood throughout: wooden and wretched looking, passing each picture, from wall or drawer or table, him to

me—formally, lifelessly—as though the two of us were partners in some awful rite. I ached for him. I'd never before seen
a parent's love so raw.

"He was a beautiful boy" was all I could summon. "You
must be very proud."

He seemed not to hear.

"Happiness," he was saying now, his head tilted over a
photo he held in one hand: the five of them together, backed by
the blue of a New Hampshire lake, close bunched and smiling
under a summer sky.

"Happiness," he said again, still seeming not to know or
care that I was there. *"That's* happiness."

3

Newhallville, the neighborhood that is home to Jim and Julia Fleming, their three children, three grandchildren, unnumbered nieces and nephews, and roughly a fourth of New Haven's blacks—perhaps ten thousand people in all—is the unlikeliest ghetto I have ever seen. There are no projects or tenements, or rusted-out car hulks, or overturned garbage in the streets. In their place: convenience stores, laundromats, wood-frame Baptist churches, a "Neighborhood Watch" sign on every tenth or twelfth block. The sidewalks, more or less, are clean. Here and there, an elm or sumac, planted years ago by the city, grows healthy and straight to the sky.

New Haven has more than its share of gutted-out slums. In

both the Elm Haven projects in the Dixwell section and in Quinnipiac Terrace across town, the poverty is as abject and visible as any in America. Driving the streets of those sections (you would not want to walk them, at least not alone) is an object lesson in apathy and despair.

Newhallville, next to those, seems an Eden. The houses, to begin with, are mostly all wood: two- and three-family row homes built nearly a century ago, in faded pastels, with windows point-blank to the windows of the houses next door. Some, perhaps a fifth, are sagging now and boarded up, though just as often there is a gay-colored plant near the door front or a fresh coat of paint on the porch.

But the signs are there. You need only look twice to see. On winter midafternoons, the fifth- and sixth-graders from the Martin Luther King Middle School on Dixwell Avenue, on their way home to expectant mothers, will outnumber—just briefly —the boys in their teens and early twenties who cluster, loose-lipped and familiar, with the false swagger of recruits under fire, at the corners of every fourth or fifth block. Half an hour later, the children safely home, the streets will belong to the pushers again—who, once darkness has fallen, with a frequency that (residents will tell you) runs more or less in spurts, will make the night ring with their gunshots and tire screams and the squawks from the beepers they carry hitched to their belts.

The first time I drove the Newhallville streets at night, I was as skittish as a deer: doors latched, windows up, eyes to the sides as much as ahead. I learned soon, though, that I had little to fear. A white man in a car is a hopeful sign for these boys: At every fourth or fifth light, I catch an eye with a hand below it that offers a shiny bag. I shake my head and drive on.

Neighborhood mothers, fearful for their families and knowing there is no help to be had, will call for it anyway—as Julia Fleming has done more times than she can count.

"With the police," she says—and makes a face like a prune —"it always goes the same. But what you gonna do?

" 'They's shootin' out here,' I tell 'em—'these kids, they's shootin' again, you gotta send a car . . .'

" 'Name, address, phone number?'—they always ask the same . . .

" 'What you wanna know all that for?' I ask 'em—'I tell you, they's shootin' in the street.'

" 'How many is shot?' they wanna know then.

" 'What? You want me to go out there and do a *count?* I told you already, they's kids bein' shot outside.'

"Half the time, they don't come at all. Other half, they come, ride by, never get outta their cars. They scared, like everybody else. Ain't gonna do no good anyways. It's the kids, these days, be runnin' the streets. . . ."

At the spot they call the Mudhole, a vacant, rubble-choked lot off Shelton Avenue that straddles a disused railroad track, the Friday night traffic is almost nonstop. Mustangs, Volkswagens, Firebirds, BMWs, Audis, Saabs, at least one flawless, fifties-era, spanking white MG—young and old, white and black, from the suburbs and the city.

They drive by, ogling, not much faster than a walker's pace; maybe circle the block a time or two (the police, though always close by, aren't apt to interfere), then catch an eye and pull over to the curb. Bags are exchanged for dollars through open windows in the time it takes to shake hands—and the cars, no longer poking, pull away.

"You got sixty-, seventy-year-old people out here doin' drugs," Julia Fleming says. "I'm talkin' senior citizens now . . .

"These two fat old white ladies—they about *this* big, the two of 'em, they take up the whole front seat of the car—they come through here all the time, right on the corner out there. They get their stuff, and away they go. . . ."

It hasn't always been this way. When Julia Fleming lived here as a teenager in the fifties and early sixties—she'd come north with two sisters, to live with an uncle after her mother in the South took sick—Newhallville was a proud, thriving neighborhood of "good people who worked hard, went to church Sundays, and brought their kids up right.

"They was Irish people, Italian people, Jews, Puerto Ricans —everybody just livin' together and not thinkin' 'bout it twice. . . . I believe, at one time or other, we was the only black family on the block. . . ."

Many, if not most of them, worked for the same employer: Olin Industries, a manufacturer of brass and ammunition whose plant at the end of Newhall Street was the neighborhood's anchor. The Olin workforce, at the time of Julia Fleming's arrival as a thirteen-year-old in the summer of 1957, was upward of six thousand people. There were a half-dozen other plants, in or near New Haven, of the same general size; the city's unemployment rate was barely 5 percent.

The boom had peaked, more or less, in the war years—then

began eroding, at first so faintly it could scarcely be felt. But
by the mid- to late fifties, the slippage had begun for real:
layoffs, factory closings, "white flight" to the suburbs, the bur-
geoning of a welfare class. In 1981, when the Olin plant
ceased operations, it employed just over a thousand workers—
roughly a sixth of its workforce of thirty years before.

Between 1950 and 1988, while the city's population
dropped by more than a quarter—to 122,000—the number of
blacks increased fivefold. There are roughly 50,000 in New
Haven today, nearly all of them poor, unskilled, underedu-
cated, or unemployed—often all of these, and with a rap sheet
to boot. "Real unemployment," citywide, is said to be 30 percent. Among young blacks, it may be half again this high. In
the city in 1989, according to government figures, more than
one person in five lived below the poverty line. It is almost
certainly worse than that today.

And for the next generation, there is even less hope: Fewer
than a tenth of the students in New Haven's black ghettos,
according to the results of a 1990 test, read at or above grade
level; among white suburban students, the percentage is three
out of four. The dropout rate among the city ninth- through
twelfth-graders is the highest in the state.

But for all that, Jim Fleming will tell you, when he arrived in
New Haven from Baltimore in 1979, "It was still a pretty decent place to be.

"Oh, they was people out there drinkin' beer and all,
and you might have a fight now and then, but nothing like
it is today. . . . Nowadays, you got people robbin' each
other, killin' each other, breakin' into churches and stealin'
stuff. . . .

"When they start breakin' into churches, you know, that says for sure that times are bad. . . ."

If there was some moment or hour, some single defining point when the forces of change took their final turn against New Haven, you might say it came on the day when the first young black boy died for cocaine.

There's no telling when that was exactly—sometime in the mideighties, no doubt. Or who he was—he might have been a "work boy" dealing capsules in a hallway, or a "piss boy" working customers in the street. He could have been a 'Ville Boy, a Latin King, an Island Brother—or an addict, or a boy on his way to school caught in a cross fire between gangs. He may have lived in Newhallville or Kensington or the Q Terrace projects. He was probably no older than sixteen.

In New Haven, between 1985 and 1991, the number of murders each year almost tripled, from twelve to thirty-four. Assaults doubled—to two thousand—while robberies increased by half. The city's overall crime rate (14,900 per 100,000 population) is greater than that of Washington, Detroit, Dallas, or New York. Forty percent of New Haven's ghetto schoolchildren, according to a survey in the summer of 1992, have witnessed a murder before they turn fifteen.

There are those who argue that drugs are not the cause: that to blame them for the carnage is like blaming an alcoholic's misery on the whiskey he drinks. The real issue, they say, is poverty—and the ignorance, desperation, and false values that it breeds.

That may be. It's certainly true that poor black boys sell more drugs than rich white ones. But it's begging the question.

Where there is poverty, there are drugs—and in New Haven, ever since the times turned bad, it's never been hard to find ways to get high. Heroin, at least since the sixties, has been a staple of ghetto life. Acid and speed had their day. As for "reefer," it's hard today to find a black boy over fourteen who even views it as a drug. "More like a 'cocktail,' " one of them told me. "You smoke it to ease down."

"Nostalgia is rampant in black New Haven," William Finnegan wrote in *The New Yorker* in September of 1990, in a two-part series detailing the city's woes. "Even the junkies in New Haven are nostalgic. They recall a camaraderie, a time when dealers were just supporting their own habits, when there was little violence, and drugs were advanced to users who could not pay. . . ."

But cocaine—the "Little White Horse." Cocaine is something else. It has hit this town like bootleg liquor hit Chicago ("Drug Violence Reminiscent of Prohibition," read a local headline in early 1992). In the space of two years—between 1985 and 1987, give or take six months on either side—it created an industry: buyers, dealers, piss boys, work boys, five thousand addicts in the city alone, thousands more in the suburbs; tens of millions of dollars a year going from jeans pockets to BMWs, Air Jordans, and gold chains; lawyers, bondsmen, jewelers, and car dealers with paid-down mortgages and private-school kids.

Most of it, at least until recently, has been bought and sold in powder form—ten-dollar capsules or bags. Users could either snort it straight, mix it with water and inject it with a needle, or cook it up and smoke it as crack. (Street crack, which was displacing powder as the big-city drug of choice as early as the late eighties, has been slow to take hold in New Haven.)

There are stories, most of them true. The sneakers store in

the mall that posted a sign—"Drug Dealers, Stay Away, We Don't Want Your Business"—and was out of business within nine months. The ghetto dry cleaner who was facing foreclosure because six out of ten of his customers weren't bothering to pick up their clothes—they just bought new ones instead.

Fantastic, incalculable dollars are being made. Fourteen-year-olds routinely earn $300 in an afternoon, sometimes much more. The distributors—the boys at the top, and few are over nineteen—net $8,000 and up for a single round-trip to New York. None of it is bankable; almost none of it is saved. The only two downsides are jail and death.

There are perhaps a dozen "posses" in New Haven. Their chief purpose is to sell drugs—and to protect their right to sell them on the turf they've marked out as their own. The 'Ville works Newhallville, the Island Brothers run Church Street South, Kensington belongs to KSI. From time to time, there are alliances—the Island, at least as this is written, is allied with the 'Ville—other times mutations. More often, there are wars.

Guns, by a wide margin, are the weapons of choice, though particular preferences vary. Twenty-twos, twenty-fives, and thirty-eights are the most common; semiautomatics, as a rule, are preferred over revolvers, though sawed-off shotguns are also among most posses' caches. Popular brand names include Sundance, Bryco, RG, Intertec, and Smith & Wesson.

In New Haven between 1989 and 1991, there were 1,162 shootings, a little more than one a day. Ninety-nine were fatal, including that of Christian Prince. Roughly 75 percent of the victims were black.

More recent figures, as of this writing, have yet to be released, though it doesn't seem likely—judging from recent local headlines and six o'clock news reports—that they're going to reverse any trends:

In January 1993, three students from the same high school, in separate incidents two weeks apart, died of gunshot wounds.

In late 1992, a five-year-old was caught in a cross fire between posses; he was shot in the mouth but survived—the second kindergartner in ten months to take a bullet intended for a member of a rival gang. The first was on her way to school, shot through the windows of a bus.

In October 1992, three members of the Latin Kings were shot and killed on a baseball field—"execution style," the paper said—by Eddie "Loco" Hernandez, another member of the gang. The three, reportedly, had attempted to resign.

How many of your friends would you say have died?" I ask Dunc's sister Tanya. She has just turned nineteen.

"Not all friends, exactly—some of 'em friends, the rest just people I know."

"About how many would you say?"

"Lots."

"You miss them? You think about them much?"

"Some that die, I miss them—but they chose to do what they do. I really got nothin' to say."

"Have you been to many funerals?"

"Don't go to funerals no more. Not since Taz. He was like my big brother—when he died, Dunc and me, we cried our eyes out behind the building, cried till there was no more cryin' to do. . . .

"Two weeks later, my uncle died—I couldn't cry a tear.

"So that's why I don't go to funerals no more."

4

He was an unexceptional child: the youngest, shyest, and un-
surest of the three. "An eight-year-old standing in the corner,
almost afraid to look at you," a family friend recalls.

"We would like to see him become more outgoing," his father would write of him on his application to prep school,
where the headmaster would find him to be "shy, reluctant,
uncertain of his intellectual bent."

He had no special gifts. His academic promise, as recalled
by the same headmaster (Josiah Bunting of the Lawrenceville
School), was "sound but not unusual." As a sophomore athlete
—football, hockey, lacrosse, most of it in backup roles—he
showed less brilliance than pluck.

He was a boy of high privilege but only average talents. The
sort of boy, like so many thousands of other prep schoolers

before and since, you'd expect to muddle through college, move seamlessly into a trainee's spot with the family firm, then marry docilely at twenty-five, only rarely to be heard from again.

But he wasn't like those boys. He studied longer. He practiced harder. In his dreams, which weren't of docile things, there was no allowance made for lack of gifts. His life, as untimely-ended as it was, was a stubborn, nearly tireless act of will.

"He was ferocious," a teammate wrote in a letter to his parents a month after he died. "[Even at practice], the damn kid would play you all the way out on the sideline, always slapping and poking, never giving you a moment's peace, daring you to drive the cage on him. . . . He was tenacious, he never quit."

By his senior year at Lawrenceville, Christian Prince was a three-letter athlete and all-American lacrosse player, a Dean's List student, the Most Improved Football Player, an editor of the school paper, president of his dorm, vice president of the school, and winner of the Sullivan Award for Manliness and Sportsmanship.

"It was a case of just *total* commitment," recalls Jim Adams, then Christian's dorm counselor, today assistant headmaster of the school. "A combination of reasonable gifts and remarkable character. He was one of those kids who just *emanated* character. The others gravitated to him."

Adams tells the story of another boy, a classmate of Christian's: a "shy, tortured kid" who risked expulsion and disgrace because of an alcohol problem so advanced he was "getting high three times a day, couldn't talk to girls without the help of booze."

It was Christian, Adams says, who "took the boy on"—earned his trust, convinced him to go public with his problem, then to seek the help he needed. And after that, when the boy returned to the school after six weeks of rehab ("a complete turnaround, one of those success stories that make this job worthwhile"), it was Christian, again, who led the move to keep him straight.

"I've been here sixteen years, I've known a lot of boys. He was one of the rare ones, a genuinely good, truly remarkable kid. He had a maturity way beyond his years, an instinctive sense of right and wrong. . . .

"He was *formed* already at sixteen. His values were intact—you could literally *see* him as an adult."

Josiah Bunting, in a eulogy delivered only days after his former student's death, put the message more loftily, though its essence was pretty much the same. And there is that word again:

"He had that most underestimated of rare commodities—he had character. The simple habit of always doing what's right, of carrying out the things you believe in, no matter how long it takes or how absent the world's applause . . .

"His code of life was [basic]—'I'll take what I'm given by the Lord, make the best of it, act always on conscience, think about myself last, and not worry too much about the consequences. . . .'

"Our culture would call this homely. I call it greatness."

Chevy Chase, Maryland, is a rarefied place to grow up. There is no hunger here, or homelessness, or street crime, or human misery of any sort you can touch or see. Skin color, except in backyards and kitchens, is mostly all white.

On Longfellow Place and the streets and roads that sur-

round it, the lawns and fairways are wide and rolling and lovingly tended. On summer nights, the smells of steaks from
poolside patios mix pleasingly with the careless cries of
splashing girls and boys. In the taproom of the Chevy Chase
Club, adjacent to the eighteenth green, twenty-five minutes by
car from the grittiest of Washington's black ghettos, surgeons
and stockbrokers trade stories of their sons' and daughters'
small misadventures at Lawrenceville or Groton or Woodberry
Forest or Saint Paul's.

Christian Prince passed his childhood here: contented, days
filled, world widening, wanting for nothing at all. He had a
paper route. He mowed lawns, shoveled snow, and caddied for
his father's friends. On fourth-grade mornings, on his way to
school in the backseat of the family car, he'd sit quietly ("taking it all in," his mother remembers today) as the other, older
boys—his brother Teddy and friends—joked and bantered
about sports and girls and teenage boy–things.

"Gettin' any lately, little brother?" Teddy Prince would
tease him, and he would laugh softly and say nothing but know
in his heart that his day would soon come.

He grew up quickly. "We have a detention book," he wrote,
as a nine-year-old, to his sister Jackie, by then a freshman at
Yale. "But I haven't signed it yet." He took clarinet lessons,
did his homework on computer. By ten, for all his shyness, he
was vice president of his class.

Few childhoods were ever more sunny. A sister to talk to, a
brother to worship, a neighborhood of schoolmates who lived to
play games. Through the winters and early springs of the golf-
ers' off-season, they had the run of the fairways of the Colum-
bia Country Club: soldier games, Cowboys and Indians, a little
boys' Elysium. In mid-May, the tarp would come off the pool

out back and suppers would move, almost ritually, like Christmas coming, out of doors.

And as time passed, and teenage years brought the need for manlier things: golf games and tennis tournaments, summerleague lacrosse, a windsurfer and Sunfish in the boathouse of the family's New Hampshire lakeside second home. A week at a Colorado dude ranch, two weeks in the Swiss Alps, summerlong canoe trips under the tutelage of Camp Waban counselors paddling and portaging the length of Hudson Bay.

Many families are as blessed. My own was one of them. Many boys spend their teenage winters at boarding schools as I did, their summers in second homes, private camps, or on eightweek canoe treks across Ontario or Quebec. Through such "advantages," now as then, wealthy young boys come to learn —or so the thinking goes—the outlines and expectations of their world. To become, in their fashion, men.

But for too many such children—though not for Christian, Teddy, or Jackie Prince—their boarding schools *are* their homes; their teachers and camp counselors the surrogates for the parents they only barely know. A father's baseball mitt gathers dust in the attic; a mother's bedtime readings become fewer, then lapse, then stop. Checks are written. A child is put on a plane. Parents, over time, change to strangers. Privilege becomes—insidiously, masking itself as love—a license for neglect.

Not so in the Prince family. As a child growing up in this household, in this boxy, hodgepodge, sun-filled home on

Longfellow Boulevard, with its overstuffed rooms and ram-
bling, run-on kitchen, and its crazy-quilt basement stacked
with old tennis trophies and split-shafted golf clubs—the bathroom walls papered with cartoon figures of gangsters and their
molls—these are the things you would know, and come to
count on, and take with you when you left:

. . . A pert, pretty mother who was seldom off her feet, who
preached frugalness in the midst of plenty, overcooked your
burgers while she beat on the base of a bottle of salad dressing
for the last available drop, talked endlessly of projects you
thought wildly improbable but more often than not then saw
done, lectured you sternly about the "unacceptable behavior"
of a selfish act but was an easy mark for a third-grader with a
tummy ache on a schoolday morning; who made care packages
for the homeless at Christmas, took the "liberal" side at din-
ner-table talks, would pass up meals to drag you to museums,
and before your bedtime every night would "read and read and
read."

She was the mother all your friends loved—who fed them
and played their games and drove them in the mornings to
school. But her heart, you knew, was yours alone. And in the
end it would break with the pain.

. . . An old-fashioned father whose old-fashioned values
were the butt of family jokes, who could laugh at them as
easily as you could, but expected no laughter when the time
came for charity or diligence or getting home on time; who
would insist, at a party, that you make friends with the shyest
child there; who played golf and tennis with a passion for
winning you couldn't help but adopt ("Dear Christian . . .
Your first job when you get home will be to work on your
paddle tennis"), was quietly religious, more loudly Republi-
can, saw through the ruses your mother fell prey to—but would

toss a ball with you when you were barely out of diapers ("big balls, little balls, whatever they could hold"), miss a partners' meeting to watch your Peewee games—then ride the team bus back with you and buy a Big Mac and fries for every boy on it.

. . . And the two of them together. And the three of you. Suppers in the dining room or by the pool, summers at the lake. The family trip to Switzerland in the winter of 1989. Father-son tournaments, Parents' Day at school. The time they both showed up to watch you play the Big Game, and most of all you did was shuttle in plays: "Sally, watch carefully and you'll see Christian running in and out on every other play. That's your son, Sally, he's the one who runs in and out."

As a sixth-grader at the Landon School, he was not a promising student: "Christian continues to put forth a good effort but not his best. As of late he has been most inattentive in class. . . . His final exam was disappointing. He must change his attitude toward his work before he can progress any farther. . . ."

Ted Prince, Sr., sat his son down. He neither punished nor threatened. He told him (as nearly as he can recall today) that he remembered having had some troubles himself paying attention in class as a child, that Christian was "a bright boy who could do better"—that he was "disappointed" but didn't expect to remain that way. By the next report card, there was only one grade below an A.

Yet through it all—somehow—he remained disorganized, impulsive, careless of money, often sloppy in his work. He remained a boy. And for all his drive and diligence, he never forgot what it meant to have fun: "When it's three A.M. and we still feel like gettin' down," he wrote, impishly, to his big sister only days before his death, "we listen to Clifton Cheneer [*sic*] and the Zydermen and 'Room Full of Blues.' . . . Last weekend was a blast—skied all day, mainly partied all night. . . . Thanks a lot for the CDs."

And there was another side, too, to this boy. Like his mother, who'd once spent her mornings in a home for poor families on Washington's south side, he seemed to understand (as so few of his kind ever do) that the privilege of birth was not a license to look the other way. He had compassion.

There are a dozen stories that prove this: his alcoholic classmate, the afternoons he gave to Montgomery County Hunger Relief, the summer project he had planned but never lived to see—to help rescue a tribe of Quebec's Cree Indians from the advances of a hydroelectric plant. But one, for its simple poignance, stands out above the rest:

Halfway through the reception that followed Christian's memorial service in New Haven—a reception that included, among others, college deans and faculty, roommates, family, and friends—a black man perhaps twice his age, in a cheap, illfitting, mismatched suit, arrived at the door. He was uninvited and declined—no doubt out of embarrassment for his clothes and the color of his skin—to join the guests inside. He wanted only, he said, a moment of some family member's time. It was brother Teddy who came forward to greet him at the door.

He had known Christian Prince, he said. The two of them had shared breakfasts together—more or less regularly, at some little coffee shop in town—the fall and winter before he died. They'd exchanged confidences; had become, in some way, friends. He didn't say—he may have been too proud, and Teddy never asked—who it was who'd picked up the checks those mornings.

That's all he'd come for: to say that he'd known him, and liked him, and would miss those breakfasts they'd shared.

"Keep on marchin'," he said to his brother—the last words, he told him, that Christian had said to him—then left, before Teddy had thought to ask his name.

5

Christian adored his big sister. She was the light of his life. His brother Ted was the mentor, the hero-model-protector (and later rival) through whose eyes he measured his worth in sports and school. ("Anytime I had trouble with Christian," their father says today, "I'd get Teddy to straighten him out.") But it was Jackie who most defined his days.

She was nine years older, a senior in high school by the time he reached third grade. They delighted each other.

"At first, I guess, I felt sort of like a second mom—it's exciting having a little brother, especially one so much younger, and so cute. . . .

"But things evolved—I got old enough to baby-sit, then old

enough to drive—and pretty soon I was taking him every-where. We'd go to Roy Rogers together, to Jerry's Sub Shop, to the movies on rainy days. I took him to his games, his practices, wherever he needed to go. . . . We got really close.

"I dated his hockey coach. Skeeter—I swear, that was really his name—the first serious boyfriend I ever had. He was three or four years older than me, taking a year off from col-lege, coaching the kids at the Chevy Chase Club. I was a senior in high school at the time; Christian was maybe nine or ten.

"Anyway, Skeeter had this zippy little stick-shift car—I for-get what it was—and he'd take us around in it, to lunches, on errands, wherever we were going at the time.

"Christian would show up at all his games in the coach's car —when all his friends were arriving with their moms—then leave with us, too, at the end. And Skeeter would come back to the house, and we'd all sit around drinking Cokes.

"My brother got *so* much mileage out of that—the coach's little buddy, the coolest guy on the team. I can still remember his smile. . . ."

He called his sister "Jackson"—her middle name, a kind of code for the specialness they shared. She taught him how to cook and play draw poker. They went on bike rides and overnights; she drilled him on the Endangered Species list. When she had a new boyfriend, he was often the first to know.

In the fall of 1980, two months after Christian's ninth birth-day, Jackie left home for her freshman year at Yale. The letters followed within weeks: "Dear Jackson: Homework is hard but I can handle it. I am vice president of my class. My friend taut me how to draw knights. . . . I wish you were here to take us to Jerry's Sub Shop." On the back of one was a diagram of his room.

Time and distance changed nothing. When Jackie stayed on at Yale as a grad student, her brother, in his early teens now, would arrive for the weekend and bed down on her couch—at least once causing havoc in the dorm, when he locked himself out of her room in his pajamas at six in the morning. When she finished school and took her first job—in Washington—Christian, himself by now a freshman at Yale, would arrive without warning on a Friday or Saturday night.

"I'd rarely know what day he was coming, never mind what time. He'd call from the subway station and say something like, 'Okay, I think I got off at the right stop, now how do I get there?' Twenty minutes later, he'd show up at the door, usually with about a dime in his pocket.

"He was incredible that way. He never worried about anything."

In mid-February 1991, less than a week before his death, Christian phoned his sister in Washington. There was this girl at Yale, he said. Her name was Diana. They'd been friends for a while, but now he thought—maybe—he might like it to be more. Valentine's Day was coming up. Should he send flowers, or would that be too bold?

"I told him to go for it," Jackie Prince says today. It was the last time they would talk.

My love for him was so simple, so uncomplicated. He was my little brother. He was wonderful, and I adored him—and now he's gone. . . .

"We had such an incredible family. A blessed family. I used to go to church and say, 'Thank you, God, for letting me be so lucky.' But not anymore. Now I either pray to Christian—talk to him, really—or just ask for the strength to help with the pain.

"I feel like God, or whoever He is—He's got to be crying somewhere, too. Because this sure wasn't part of any grand plan. . . ."

6

"I think at some point I sort of *kissed* Christian," Diana Montgomery tells me.

She is as pretty as she is wholesome, with straight brown hair that hangs loose to her shoulders, and intelligent, water-blue eyes that never fail to meet mine. We are sitting across from each other at a table in Atticus Books, a sprawling, too-loud bookstore/café on the fringes of the Yale campus, a dozen or so blocks from where her friend and classmate was murdered twenty-two months before. They were *close* friends, she tells me; had he lived, they might have gone on to be more.

"I knew he had a crush on me freshman year. I figured he'd gotten over it. Did you know, though—he was going to send me flowers that Valentine's Day, the [Thursday] before he died?"

Yes, I say, Jackie told me. I guess he must have lost his nerve.

"I wish he hadn't. I wish he'd gone ahead and sent them—I'd have been so *psyched!*"

She smiles, briefly and foolishly, looking for the first time like the little girl she so nearly is. Then her lip quivers, she bites it and looks away, then back. The college girl again:

"I don't want to make him sound like the perfect person. It's so easy to do that after someone dies. . . . It's just that he was—so *good,* so absolutely good."

She'd known a hundred such boys: from Groton and Saint Paul's and Deerfield, from her teenage summers in Maine. She'd known too many. They were, by her reckoning, too much the same: "Good looking, with a kind of swagger—cocky, obnoxious, you know the type. Rich, preppy white boys who think they own the world . . .

"But he was different. So different—but in so many ways the same. . . . He was smart, good-looking; he worked hard; he was a terrific athlete. I mean, just your all-around great guy . . ."

She laughs at herself now—a warm, open, half-guilty little laugh that tells me she sees the folly in what she has said.

"I know, I know. . . . But he *was* different, he really was. He was good. He was kind. He was solid. He saw—I mean really saw—how lucky he was. The advantages he had. A lot of people are corrupted by that. But not Christian. He knew what he had; it wasn't lost on him. He just worked that much harder to deserve it.

"He had such dreams. He used to talk sometimes about

doing something with the government—environmental work probably, maybe with the EDF [the Environmental Defense Fund] like Jackie does—he was so proud of her. Or even politics . . .

"I guess what I'm trying to say is—he was the *best of it*. The best of what someone like him, like us—the 'haves,' the lucky ones—are supposed to be.

"But so few of us ever make it. So few of us really are. Christian was the exception.

"I just hope he knew how much I loved him."

She rambles on, retrieving memories: the day they'd met as freshmen, the classes and projects and pizzas they'd shared, the weekend together skiing in Vermont with a houseful of friends, only three weeks before his death—"I felt like we were getting closer then"—his smile, his easy greeting ("Hey, Diana, what's up?"), the sun-dried tomatoes he'd liked to cook for pretty girls.

And finally, about how she'd seen him that last night at Mory's, then later at the party at Strathcona Hall, only minutes before he died.

"For the longest time I didn't know how it had been. . . . Had he been found there in the morning? Had he lain there on the sidewalk for hours—all alone, but sort of conscious? Had it happened quick or slow? Had he been in pain?

"What had been going through his mind then? Through the mind of that guy who shot him?

"I mean, what *could* go through your mind—anybody's mind—when you could pull out a gun and pull the trigger for fifty bucks that I don't even think he got?

"That was the hardest part, for me at least. I needed to do

that, to reconstruct it. I needed to find a way to make it *real.*"

It's been nearly two years. And still it's not real. Her friend murdered in February, her mother dead of cancer the following March—the pair of losses, she says, forever linked in her mind. Neither one real, neither one fathomable. Each one, she says, "like a dream . . ."

But the worst of it: the most alien, the most dreamlike, the most unfathomable part—and here she is on the edge of breaking: "Did that boy who killed him have *no idea* that Christian was anything like him, that they were two human beings on the same street at the same time? Was there just *no sense of connection?*"

To watch this young woman, this lovely, sensitive, impeccably bred college girl (Brearly, Groton, Yale '93) from the coast of Maine and the Upper East Side of Manhattan, trying so earnestly, her voice never more than a tick away from cracking, to wrestle some shred of meaning out of the random murder of her friend—to find some "connection" of "humanness" between a suburban white boy and a poor black driven only by impotence and rage—is to understand, so visually I want to tell her so, why it is I am sitting at this little bookstore table. Why it is their story must be told.

7

For most of the summer of 1990—the last summer he would see—he was probably as happy as he'd been in his life.

He was in Fort Smith, Arkansas, loading couches onto trucks. Forty-odd trailer loads—the better part of a warehouse —over the space of ten weeks. Five hundred tons of furniture, maybe more.

He was with his best friend. Lawrence Deas ("Lawrence," never "Larry"), another classmate at Yale. But this one from Tupelo—slow talking, with a thick, rolling, Mississippi drawl, an outsized gut, and a Deep South fondness for cars and guns. Of all Christian's friends at Yale (or maybe anywhere, ever), Lawrence, you'd have to say, was the least likely.

The couches they loaded—most of them fire damaged, water damaged, or otherwise not much good—belonged to Lawrence's father, who owned a furniture company back in Tupelo and had bought them for a song. The boys' job that summer was to sort the good from the bad ("the usable from the useless"), then load them onto trucks for the ride east to Mississippi. They worked nine hours a day, five days a week (except sometimes on Fridays), and hired any help that walked in the door at four dollars an hour. On weekends, usually, they raised whatever hell they could find.

"We shot a lot of pool, drank a lot of beer, lifted a lot of couches, and sweated a lot" is how Lawrence remembers those weeks.

"Basically, we were the only ones either of us knew in the town. We shared a one-bedroom apartment and took turns sleeping on the couch. That's a pretty damn-sure way to get to know somebody. . . ."

He is sitting across from me at the same little bookstore table I'd shared a week before with Diana Montgomery. He is large, both around and up-and-down, with soft eyes, an open face, and an easy, generous way you could spot across a room. He's wearing a dark blue windbreaker—Yale Skeet—with crossed rifles across one breast, and a red Marlboro Racing Team baseball cap. I like him instantly.

"We had this huge old 1977 teal blue, beached-out Lincoln Town Car. It drove like a damn *boat*. We'd close up the warehouse early Friday afternoon, point it straight for Little Rock, and party all weekend."

It takes us awhile to get down to talking about Christian. It's a tough subject for him, even after two years.

"I'm real angry," he tells me. "I'll probably always be angry."

After it happened, he says, he was too angry even to cry. So he never did. "I watched a lot of other people cry. I couldn't— I was just too mad. The anger kept it from hurting. But I never got to cry. . . ."

Then he tells me he has a gun.

"Somebody tries to hurt me, I'm gonna *kill* 'em. I wouldn't hesitate. I wouldn't think twice."

His fists are clenched when he says this. His eyes are narrowed and turned away. He wants revenge. It's been two years —and still he wants revenge.

"I read in the paper that it'd been sixteen years since the last Yale kid was killed. . . . It won't be another sixteen years. You watch—somebody else's going to get killed, this year or next. . . .

"There's too much damn bitterness out there, too much anger. There's gunshots all the time."

Are you scared? I ask him.

"*Damn* scared sometimes," he says. "But I'll be ready."

Something about these two boys—the northern WASP, the wild-ass, irreverent Mississippian who'd rather fight than shed tears—appealed to one another. Lawrence Deas didn't know lacrosse from horseshoes; the first time he tried to ski (with Christian as his guide), he damn near strangled himself with a six-foot scarf.

One was almost bullish, the other almost shy. One was shaped in a redneck culture ("On some level, I can't help being a good ol' boy—it's kind of hard to just kick those values aside"), the other by the codes and norms of an eastern prep school. In a hundred ways, they were as different as two young men could be.

But they liked each other. They were crazy about each other. They were going to room together junior year.

"There was no bullshit with Christian," Lawrence tells me now. "He was one of the few people I ever knew who could tell you exactly what he thought, either way, without ever causing bad feelings. I never really saw him get mad. He was upbeat but tough at the same time—a kind of *hard* niceness."

As for what Christian saw in his Mississippi friend—Diana Montgomery, in a letter to the dead boy's parents, probably came as close as anyone could: "That first time I saw him, on the steps of Wright Hall. . . . He was so cute—shy and quiet —but wanting Lawrence's wildness to rub off on him a bit."

For all the rich summers of Christian Prince's life—the canoe trips and dude ranches, the hockey camps, the small fanfare as a volunteer in the Bush campaign—if he were alive today, I'm pretty sure he'd say that Fort Smith in 1990 was the richest. Or at least, like the friend he spent it with, the rarest, the most different:

"It was so far away from the world he'd known, from *anything* he'd known," says Lawrence. "He really let his hair down that summer; he got away from that need he always had, or always seemed to have, to please everybody in sight. . . .

"He opened up. He opened up a lot. Christian [typically] was a pretty private guy.

"He had this way about him—he'd give you this strange, skewed, off-the-wall answer anytime you ask him about anything personal, anything that really matters, like about his family or something. Then he'll smile at you sideways—like he knew you knew it was bullshit, like he's putting *it* off without putting *you* off, you know what I mean?

"It's hard to describe—but I felt like I got behind that wall a little that summer, like I found out some things maybe no one else knew. . . ."

From time to time as the hour goes by, as the memories of his friend grow more personal, Lawrence slips back and forth between tenses—past, then present, then past again—as though he can't make up his mind somehow whether Christian's qualities died with him, whether the mysteries that were unraveled to him that summer in Fort Smith were part of some higher truth that has survived its bearer.

"There was this sense you got with Christian, that he's blindly following some track—the prep school–Ivy League–lawyer track—that it's all laid out, nice and neat, like with his father.

"It was never really that way. I mean, he saw the advantages he had; he never apologized for his background. But he saw the ridiculousness of it, too—he saw that it wasn't the real world.

"He looked at things differently than his father. Differently than Teddy. His vision of the world was more in line with his sister's—with the kind of idealism she brought to things.

"I mean, he definitely wasn't going to sit in a law firm and handle contracts all day for the rest of his life."

One thing grows clearer the longer we talk: Lawrence is telling me far less than he knows. Specifics are being generalized, confidences presented vaguely, more as inference than fact.

Some of what his friend must have said to him that last summer, I can plainly see, was not meant for any ears but his. He is torn now between loyalty and truth.

Never more so than when the subject is Christian's father. "That's a shady area for me to get into" is most of what he'll say—his voice dropping, his hands beating a sudden rat-tat-tat on the table between us—the first time I bring it up.

"Let's just say it was real, real important for him to please his dad."

Was it *too* important, do you think?

"I won't touch that" is all he says.

I ask it another way.

"Let's just stick to Christian," he says. And so we do . . .

He was trying to find his own way, his own track. Some way to blend it all together—law, the environment, his father's hopes, that idealism his sister had—to come up with something that worked for *him*.

"I guess I think that somewhere inside that world of family relationships, somewhere in there with the all those hopes and successes and big expectations, lay the answer to that need he had to be so private. . . .

"He was *looking* for himself. There's no guarantee that if he were still alive today, that he'd have figured it out yet—he had an awful lot to live up to. He'd still be looking, probably. But he'd be closer."

All this was in late December: a week before the second Christmas his friend would miss. We talked for a while about that—about how hard Christmas was for the Princes, how the first year after Christian was killed they couldn't even bring themselves to buy a tree.

Lawrence hadn't known that. He hadn't seen them or talked to them since the day they'd buried their son. He'd *wanted* to, he tells me—he'd *meant* to—he just couldn't bring himself to go.

"I've actually been in the neighborhood, I've been within a few miles of their place. I turned back, I turned chicken—like some little kid. I was afraid I wouldn't know how to act. . . .

"I mean, the only time I ever really knew them [at the funeral] was the worst time of their life. I was afraid that was the only way I'd know how to relate. I didn't want to do that. I figured they wouldn't either—so I just didn't go at all.

"Which is no excuse. I feel lousy about it. I probably ought to try again. . . ."

Four days later, on his way home for Christmas, Lawrence paid a visit to the Princes in Chevy Chase. And after that, to Christian's grave.

And then in March, ten weeks later, at the trial of the boy accused of taking his friend's life, he saw Ted Prince again.

That was the last time, as far as I know—though they plan, they've both said, to stay in touch.

8

It's almost winter again. Another Christmas only eight weeks away. Lawrence graduated last June, as you would have also, along with Diana and your roommate Jim Williams, and the last of the lacrosse team that dedicated its season to you.

The students at Yale still talk about you sometimes—"the Christian Prince killing," "that Prince kid who got shot in 'ninety-one"—but the ones who knew you all are gone. Scattered. Some to jobs, some to law school or med school, or a Fulbright year abroad. You would be a stranger at Yale today.

It's been three years, Christian. What do they remember of you? What do they say of you now?

"One of my best friends in college got murdered."

By now, more than one of them have said that: to a date or a girlfriend, or just someone new over lunch.

"Shot down in the street one night and left to die—some black ghetto kid, some scumbag with nothing else to do. No money, no motive, no reason at all."

"How awful," she might have answered. "That must have been so hard for you."

"Terrible. A total waste. The guy had so much to live for. One of the greatest human beings I ever knew."

They will talk of you this way. More and more as time goes by. You will grow dimmer in their minds as the young man you were, clearer as a symbol. As a martyr, even. Memory will be dulled by "meaning." You will grow larger as you grow less real.

The Christian Prince Memorial Lacrosse Trophy (Lawrenceville), the Christian Prince Memorial Scholarship Fund (Yale). Your name invoked by friends of your father on the floors of Congress in support of some handgun bill.

And finally, inevitably, next year or the year after or ten years from now: "[John Doe], shot in the back from a passing car on his way home from a party late Friday night, is the first Yale student to be murdered on the campus since Christian Prince in the winter of 1991."

And meanwhile the holly trees will grow thicker behind your grave, the lettering on your tombstone ("Scholar, Athlete, Leader, Friend") will grow smoother, more weathered—more like your grandmother's alongside it—until, inevitably, five years or a decade from now, the Christmas will come when there will be no flowers, no footprints in the snow.

And Lawrence and Diana and the others will work, and marry, and have children (perhaps even lose a child and learn the grief

*your parents suffer now), and grow grayer and hopefully more
wise, and pay down mortgages, and begin to notice that the
funerals they are attending are growing less far between—
though at the beginning, at the first one or two, they will no
doubt think of yours.*

*You will become, so slowly that no one will notice, the echo of
what was once a shout: Christian, Christian Prince . . . I
think at one point I sort of kissed him. . . . We lifted a lot of
couches, and sweated a lot. . . . He was the best of it. . . .
So absolutely good.*

*But one thing, Christian, one thing will not grow dim with
time. For the young men and women who knew you, and for
many more who did not, it will be remembered always, years
after all the rest is gone: The loudest and saddest message of
your life and loss. Your legacy. Not one you would have chosen,
though for that you can't be blamed.*

*Five thousand young Yale men and women who walked those
same streets every day, with bookbags and backpacks, on their
way to classes, fraternities, playing fields, the future—as mind-
less and innocent as you were that night—woke up the next
morning to a colder, meaner world. A realer world—though few
of them, at least in those first days, could have brought themselves to call it that.*

*Scores of your schoolmates, awash in their own impotence
and with nowhere else to turn, poured their anguish on your
parents: angry, misplaced letters whose rage at their just-robbed
innocence crowded sympathy from the page. "We feel raped,"
wrote one. "Violated," said another. "Sick," "disgusted," "horri-
fied"—"When we talk about Christian, we talk about revenge."*

Your death changed these people. Frightened them, hardened them. At least briefly, for that first few weeks of numbed, distracted days, it brought them closer (God forbid, for this was Yale) to the mind and heart of the "animal" who had shot you down. They learned, most for the first time in their brief, protected lives, how short can be the distance between the campus and the street.

Even Lawrence. Your best friend. He owns a gun today. Anybody messes with him, he says: "I'm gonna kill 'em. . . . I wouldn't think twice.

"Nobody I knew ever died that way before. It changed everything; it changed the way I look at things. I know now—bad stuff is going to happen. Lousy, ugly stuff you're not going to be able to stop or change, or even understand. . . .

"I'm a lot colder person today."

It's a sad judgment on our world that there could ever be a "lesson" in the murder of a nineteen-year-old boy. But this, though you would not have wanted it, has been the lesson in yours.

As many lives as you touched, as wonderfully well as you filled your nineteen years—it is this, in the end, that will be remembered and told.

We are all colder persons today.

9

He was his mother's third child, the family baby. Normal sized and healthy and almost on time. It should have been an easy birth.

Instead it nearly killed them both.

"It took darn near three days," Julia Fleming remembers. "His feet was gonna come out first. They had to push him back up there and turn him 'round—didn't want him to choke hisself to death."

Other memories are less distinct. And harder to come by. Like photos left too long in the sun, they seem, oddly, to have faded. It is as though James Fleming's childhood, not so long since passed, had been somehow compressed in the minds of those who watched or shared in it—parents, sisters, James himself; as though the years of teething and toddling and third-grade mischief had passed, miraculously, in a week or a month, leaving only the barest imprint, hardly more than a shadow, as a record of itself.

But what *else?* I ask his parents. What else can you recall? His toys, his friends, his favorite things to do—was he close to his sisters, did he leave his room a mess?

Day after day it goes like this. For a week of mornings, at intervals over two months, against the soundless backdrop of a console TV—*All My Children, Hollywood Squares*—James Senior and Julia Fleming sit at opposite ends of their living room, the mother chain-smoking Pall Malls, the father digging absently at the ghost of his missing left leg—sifting for memories that seem, incredibly, to have died.

"He was a good boy," James Fleming says vaguely. "An average boy, never no A student or nothin'. But he was never, y'know, no trouble, either—just hung with the wrong crowd, is all."

Like any child, his father remembers (it's the most he's remembered so far), young James was a sucker for TV: "He used to come into our room in the mornings, just snuggle up tight 'tween his mama and me—his little head at the bottom, peekin' out from 'tween our feet. Why, I'd wake up to those cartoons darn near every day."

James Senior smiles, a thin, odd little smile, as he recalls this. Then it is gone, just as quickly, and the blankness returns.

It is always this way: with James, with Julia, with young James himself. There is no *weight* to these memories, no joy or pride or nostalgia, no particular sadness or pain. Nothing—less than nothing—to hold them in place. And so, unweighted, they simply drift away.

It is the same whatever we talk of: James's family, or Julia's, or courtship times, or the early years before children arrived. They don't remember. Or half remember, or remember, then change their minds. Two years become three, then five, then two again. Details are blurred, then vanish entirely; dates are forgotten or reversed. The landmarks keep shifting, if they are landmarks to begin with. There is no sense of history—and without it, it seems, almost no sense at all.

I barely know these people. They are black and poor. I am white and have been broke—but never poor. I have a son—the same age, roughly, as theirs. His life: his birth and birthdays, graduations, soccer games, the day he learned to catch a ball —everything great and small I have been lucky enough to be present to witness, or hear about, is part of my record of him. On film, in memory, by report. It is my history as well as his. It is much of what makes me what I am. I cannot imagine being without it.

But *they* are without it. Or seem to be. With them, there is none of this. No sense of passage or triumph, of small things that loom great in remembering. The past seems a flat landscape, too dingy and unremarkable to record. I assume, knowing no different, that it has always been so.

But I am wrong. On the fourth or fifth morning, almost by accident, I learn—I am astonished—that there is a scrapbook of photos. Several, in fact. Weddings, funerals, new babies, family outings, the slow passings from diapers to pants—all there, all recorded, until just two years before. I would never have dreamed it. I would never have thought to ask.

Slowly, with effort, through our final two days, prodded on by the albums (which Julia has dug from a shelf), the stories begin to come. Young James had liked music. And dancing, and dressing up. He'd strummed on a child's guitar, ceaselessly for weeks on end, as a six-year-old, until the strings snapped and the face broke away from the frame. He'd been the house clown: an eight-year-old Michael Jackson in a pale red jumpsuit who could break-dance till his knees went weak. He'd had his grandmother's love of laughter—and of being laughed at—and his mother's off-center smile.

He had dreamed of being a policeman. It was no mystery why. His father, before he'd lost his eyesight—then his leg— was a regional security chief for the Rite Aid chain, driving daily routes between stores in New England and New York. He'd worn dark blue pants with gold piping, starched white shirts, a white policeman's hat with a gold star in the center. He was burly in those days, barrel-chested, with broad shoulders and large, muscular arms. He wore his hair long, in thick Jheri-Kurls sprouting out from under his hat to an inch above his shoulders. In most of the photos, he is wearing dark glasses. In all of them, he is smiling. Except for the curls, he could pass for a B-movie cop.

His office was in Hartford, a thirty-minute drive from home. And sometimes on weekends, or when there was no school, young James would ride with him—his father's white policeman's hat, as often as not, a tent on his six-year-old head— then watch and listen as James Senior called in payroll, took problem reports, made plans for the security of a soon-to-open store.

For the boy, over time, these missions—mythologized—became the core of the only calling he has so far ever known.

"I wanted to be just like my pops," young James says today.

He is in dark pants and gray, prison-issue sweatshirt, seated across from me at the blistered, room-length visitors' table in the reception center of Cheshire's Manson jail.

"He was, y'know, like a head security chief or somethin'. The boss of all the guards. He went all over—Detroit, Florida, anywhere you could name. It was a big job, a lotta responsibility. Like a cop or somethin', only with more people under him. *I* was gonna be like that—a cop or chief guard or somethin', like my pops. . . .

"But life, y'know, it has a way of takin' things away."

James and Julia Fleming are good people with good hearts— but not much left of anything else. Defeat hangs off them like a smell. He is fleshy now, and haggard, his policeman's burliness replaced by sags. She is gaunt and wasted, with legs as thin as sticks. But she has two of them at least; and knows, or seems to, that the burden—for now, for tomorrow, for how many months or years to come?—is largely hers to bear. She brings him pills and pillows, comes and goes with food and coffee and soiled linens and ashtrays for herself, cleans up her grandchildren's messes, provides a shoulder or elbow when her husband's crutches are not nearby. And sometimes—though rarely—gives voice to the heaviness she feels.

"I got *four* babies now," she says to me one morning. Her husband sits across from her, a half-empty plate in his lap. "And that ain't countin' the grandkids. Four babies—Tanya, Sandra, Duncan, and James."

"You mixin' yourself up," Jim Fleming answers. "You sayin' 'Duncan,' then you sayin' 'James'—you sayin' the same person twice."

"I ain't mixed up—I'm talkin' 'bout *you*."

"Oh."

■ ■ ■

If I had it all to do over again," Julia Fleming tells me one
morning when her husband is gone from the room (though
she'll disavow it the very next day), "I wouldn't have no kids."

I am surprised and tell her so. Wouldn't you be lonelier
without them? I ask.

"Rather be lonely than dead."

I don't understand. What's "dead" got to do with it? I want
to know.

"I feel that way sometimes. I feel that way *a lot.*"

The living room we sit in—it is the scene of all our morning
talks—is not a room at all but half of one: a small, squared-off
space of carpet whose boundaries are a battered couch
sheathed in plastic, the console TV—always on, often silent—
and the lumpy black recliner in which Jim Fleming spends his
days. The square's fourth side is the half-room in which the
couple sleep: a chest of drawers, a bedside table, an unmade
double bed. The carpeting is ancient and threadbare, the color
of dead leaves. The only window looks out on an alley. The
walls are nearly bare.

The sense you get is of transience—and a drabness so per-
vasive it seems alive.

Those was good times," James Senior says now. "We went
places, y'know—the whole family, 'least once a year. Disney
World, King's Dominion, some other place down there, I can't
'member the name. The bunch of us, just pack into the car and
drive—be gone a week at least, maybe more.

"Or a bus maybe, we did that once, too—one of them char-
ter things, y'know. That was 'eighty-five—I b'lieve it was
'eighty-five—the time we went to Disney World. Three days
down, three back. Stayed in a different hotel every night—

every one of 'em with a swimmin' pool, too. There's pictures of
all that, you want to see . . .

"Then come home, set right down and watch TV, me and
Julia and James and the girls—just take it easy for a while.
. . . On the weekends maybe, Julia and me, we'd rent out a
hall or a club or somethin' with a bunch of friends—never cost
more'n five dollars each—go out dancin', stay out half the
night.

"Good times, that's what we had. Nothin' much to complain
about. But then, as time went on, y'know, it just seemed like
things went bad."

There were no more family trips after Disney World in 1985—
the year diabetes claimed the retina of James Fleming's left
eye. The doctors said he shouldn't be driving. Two weeks before Christmas, he worked his last day.

New Haven's murder rate doubled in the two years after that.
Its income levels, in the same two years, declined by nearly
a third. The city, not so long before among New England's
most prosperous, was now the poorest in the state. One house
in ten was boarded up. One family in three lived in poverty.
One child in two, among blacks, was being raised by a single parent.

In Newhallville, quiet, tree-lined, and working class—the
neighborhood of Julia Fleming's childhood—the gangs were
taking over the streets. Only six years before, James Senior
remembers, the worst thing you had to worry about was a beer
drinker on a stoop. By late 1987, he says, "there was shootin'
darn near every night."

The children's curfew, always before loose-knit, in 1986

was cut in stone: nine P.M., eleven on weekends. At around the same time, the family bought a Smith & Wesson.

"I always felt, y'know, that the atmosphere I came up in and the atmosphere that is today—in life, in the way of livin'—shouldn't be all that different. People is people, I'm saying. But there's a big difference today, a big difference. People is gettin' *hurt* today.

"Comes the time, y'know, you gotta fight back. They shoot in here, they shoot at my family and don't get me first—I'm gonna start shootin' back."

In 1988 came the first grandchild: Tichelle, born to Tanya, who had just turned fifteen. Then Takara, three years later; then Terrence, born to Sandra, two months after that. Both sisters were mothers now, James Junior an uncle at thirteen. There were no weddings to mark the births, no fathers worthy of the name.

Neither new mother was employed, or sought to be. Sandra, in her twenties by then, had done two years of college and once had been a salesclerk at Ames—but had quit when the baby came. Tanya, pregnant at fourteen, never made it past ninth grade.

The household swelled to six, then eight. With each new baby, there was a jump in the food stamps, which were pooled for the family good. The welfare checks stayed with the mothers. Tanya, before the year was out, had her own TV and VCR.

In the fall of 1989, on his way to school one day, young James was jumped and threatened by members of a crosstown gang. He was shaken but unhurt. Within the month, he transferred to a second school—his fifth in nine years—a shorter walk from home.

Four or five months later, in February 1990, on his way to Kentucky Fried Chicken with two of his friends: "Me and Reese and Twizz, just walkin' up Starr Street hill—this car come up behind us, somebody yelled somethin', we started runnin'—and that's when the bullet hit."

He was shot through both legs—but was lucky, his father says today. The wounds, at least, were clean: "Just like you would take a drill and just drill both your legs together and put a bolt on the other side."

The reasons for the shooting seem unclear. "Mistaken identity," says James Senior; "an accident," says James, who claims to bear no grudge but will walk with a limp for the balance of his life.

In September of the same year, Julia Fleming, the only paycheck left in the house—$6.50 an hour making hand tools for Sears—was laid off her job when the shop she worked in blew down in a storm. Four months later came her first heart attack, to be followed by a stroke after that. Her husband's diabetes, meanwhile, had attacked his lower left leg. He stopped going to church when he could no longer wear a shoe.

Young James, through it all, had stayed in school. He was a ninth-grader now—three years removed from a fraction of his father's dream.

"My greatest ambition, the number one dream, was to have those diplomas hangin' there on my wall. Just to look at, y'know, whenever I gotta need to feel good. Their mother and me, we'd be gone by then, the kids could do what they want—but there'd be those diplomas.

"And then maybe, I used to think, when I was fifty years

old, then maybe I'd retire. Buy me a Winnebago and just travel
—Julia and me, wherever it felt good to go. I get up this
mornin' and felt the need to go someplace, y'know—I'd just go.
Kids be grown and gone by then, wouldn't have no strings
attached.

"Don't look like it's gonna work out that way, though.
Things haven't been 'xactly peaches and cream. . . ."

A lot of it, he says, has just been "the luck of the draw.
Julia's sickness, say, or the problems with my leg—can't
blame nobody for all that. Those kinda things just happen. You
just gotta pray and hope it all works out in the end."

Other things, the things that scare him most, have nothing
at all to do with luck.

"The big problem, y'know, the number one problem, is this
business with kids and guns—kids havin' guns. . . .

"Nobody's taught 'em, y'know, the value of a gun. They
know a gun will kill you, but nobody's really taught 'em—'A
Gun Will Kill You.' I don't b'lieve they get that yet.

"You see a eight-year-old, even maybe a seven-year-old,
carryin' a gun to school that's bigger than he is? You ask him
what he doin'—he say he be '*protecting* hisself.'

"That same little kid, somebody bother him? The first thing
he do is reach in his pocket—'I'm gonna kill you,' 'I'm gonna
shoot you.' Or maybe he have a knife as big as I-don't-know-
what—he be tryin' to cut you or stab you, y'know.

"That's how it is—worse all the time. The kids be gettin'
younger, the guns be gettin' bigger. You get so you're afraid all
the time. . . ."

The scrapbooks sit in a stack, a foot high or higher—no two
alike—covers half gone and pages peeling, under a sheaf of
down-turned photos that once, no doubt, were meant for their

pages. But once they come out and lie open between us—the color Kodaks in flat rows behind clear plastic strips—it is as though some black, impenetrable, low-hanging cloud has been shot through with sunlight. Familyhood, so long dulled, returns like a smile to the room.

The photos go back: Julia's old mother, dead now, a severe, thin-necked women all in black with tight silver hair and bottle-thick glasses; Julia herself at nineteen, full figured and pretty, a country girl in a pale denim dress; James as a young husband, grinning up broadly from a poker table in the basement of the family's Baltimore home, beer cans and card buddies all around; and again five years later, in New Haven by now, in blue suit and tie on a sunny Sunday morning, the door of the Mount Calvary Baptist Church thick with worshipers behind him.

There are postcards from a weekend trip, with friends, to Atlantic City in the late seventies ("Those days, we had money to blow"); pages of shots from Disney World and King's Dominion—ghost towns and bumper cars, Space Mountain, a huge inflated Mickey Mouse—a group portrait taken on one of James Senior's Sunday trips with the "Golden Stars," a local band of gospel singers with whom he'd liked to travel, though he couldn't sing a note.

In one of the last photos, taken at a party on New Year's of 1990, Julia is in a blue-and-white print blouse with pleated cotton slacks so white they seem to shine; James, in tan jacket and sporty maroon shirt, is standing next to her, his arm around her shoulders. Her arm is around his waist. They are turned toward each other, both smiling. You would guess, at a glance, that the new year loomed bright.

Two months later, their son would be shot through the legs and the unraveling would begin. They took no more pictures. The scrapbooks stayed on the shelf.

" 'Eighty-nine. That was the last good year," Julia Fleming says now. "It was all downhill after that."

James Junior, to look at, was a lovely child. Clear, chocolate skin, open face—his father's—large, oval eyes and an impish grin. His baby picture, since the day he went to jail, has hung on the wall above the couch.

Other, later ones fill the scrapbooks—some with his sisters or parents, others alone. As a four-year-old, in bright red pajamas on the living room floor, a fleet of Matchbox cars in convoy between his legs; three years later at his grandmother's, his face hovered over the frosting of a blue-and-white birthday cake; as a ten-year-old, break-dancing on the sidewalk in front of his home, lips pursed and intent, limbs a blur of motion, a small crowd of doting grown-ups circled at his back. At Disney World and King's Dominion; in dark suit and white tie on Easter morning of his ninth or tenth year, stiff and dutiful, hands clasped behind him, before or after church.

One of the last ones was taken on New Year's of 1988, two months past his thirteenth birthday. He is standing proudly— as tall as he can draw himself—in the doorway of the family living room, smiling thinly, the barest sort of smile. His face, no longer round, has begun to show a young man's handsomeness.

He is wearing tan pants and a black-and-silver Los Angeles Raiders sweatshirt—crossed swords over a helmeted head with a knife in its teeth—which hangs in folds at his waist. A dark blue baseball hat is snug on his head.

In his hands, loosely, comfortably, its stock and barrel a diagonal across his chest, is his father's .410 shotgun.

10

Several months after Christian Prince's murder, according to some who claim to know, a Latin King was shot by a 'Ville Boy at the corner of Winchester and Shelton. He staggered as far as the Oasis Lounge, made it inside, collapsed, and bled to death on the floor. The state stripped the bar's license. Twenty months later, the Oasis remains closed.

But it was open that night, February 16, 1991. A huge, graffiti-splotched, nearly windowless concrete rectangle at the heart of the Newhallville ghetto, it was a place where black youth from throughout the city came to shoot pool, play video games, dance, and listen to rap—sometimes, on weekends, with live performers. You could get most things you wanted there, and drink—if they knew you—without much proof of age. If you were in the 'Ville on a weekend night and your business on the street was done, the Oasis was the main place to be.

It was packed that night, a Saturday. A concert was planned: Roxanne Chantee, a West Coast rapper with four or five hits to her credit and a heavy following among the city's black youth. She was scheduled on stage around midnight. Her performance—its precise length and timing, those among the audience and those not—would be a point of focus in the months to come.

Mary Martin was tending bar. She would remember, sixteen months later, that she'd served Dunc Fleming a "snakebite" sometime around one. She knew the time, she said, because Roxanne Chantee had just gone off. It was an hour to closing. When it gets near closing, she'd say, and you're behind bar, you tend to notice the time. (As for Dunc's age, he was barely sixteen: "If they let him in at the door, it's on them then, not me.")

Pam Swint, too, saw Dunc at the Oasis that night. A sales-clerk at the Milford Caldor's, she was a former schoolmate of his sister's, had known him loosely for years. He'd owed her ten dollars, an old debt, she claimed, which she'd tried that night to collect. But Dunc had only smiled and walked away. All this had happened, she would say—depending on who asked her—sometime between midnight and a quarter after one.

Randy Fleming, like the others, would put Dunc at the Oasis that night. He himself, he said, though older than Dunc by more than a year, had been "too young" to get past the door. He never explained this and was never asked to try.

The two Flemings are not related. Both today are in jail: Dunc because of what happened that night—whatever happened that night—Randy because, according to witnesses, he shot a sixteen-year-old in the head a year later with a stolen twenty-two. The victim survived. Randy is awaiting trial for assault. If convicted, he could face twenty years. His life seems over before he is twenty himself.

But on that Saturday night in February, both boys were still free. And still friends—"associates" is how they say it on the street, where friendships can be fleeting. They lived a block apart, had known each other as long as either one could remember. Randy was a member of the Lynch Mob. Dunc was or wasn't, depending on whom you ask. But they hung with the same general crowd.

It was midnight, and cold—below freezing. But Roxanne Chantee had brought out a crowd. On Winchester Avenue between Ivy and Shelton, the Oasis was the center of life. Those not inside were close by: some on the street by its doors; others cruising; still others—as Randy would say he was—watching from windows that offered a view.

James Fleming, Sr., even at that late date, still held his son to curfews. Or tried to, or says he did. On weekends it was 1:00 A.M.—and Dunc, most nights, didn't have far to go. The Flemings' home, the second floor of a three-story wood row house, is next door to the Oasis Lounge.

The concert was late getting started. Sometime around midnight, Randy Fleming would say, he saw Dunc coming out of the bar "with my man, Money Russ." The street was crowded and mostly unlit—and Randy's window was half a block away —but he was sure, he said, of the faces he saw: "Lotta people, man, lotta people—'least about thirty heads. Guy named John, guy named Tony. And Dunc, too. They was all out chillin', man, in front of his house."

The last he saw of his friend that night, he would recall, was several minutes later: Dunc left the crowd, climbed the stairs, and walked into his home alone. Apparently—or so it would seem—without waiting for the concert next door to begin.

All this was said in court, under oath, sixteen months after Christian Prince was killed. If true, it would have removed any good reason to hold Dunc Fleming accountable for his death.

But there is no reason to believe it's true. Or not true. Or to believe, either, the other version Randy Fleming gave—thirteen months earlier, signed and recorded and also sworn to truth: that Dunc had *not* made his curfew that night, that with Randy and two others he'd driven a cokehead's white Nissan to the eastern edge of the Yale campus, spotted a white boy—a "cracker"—walking alone on an empty street, parked the car, robbed the boy, pistol-whipped him once across the face, then shot him—for no reason—in the heart.

So many lies have been told about that night. A hundred or more probably, if you count all the tellers and all the versions they've told. But who was lying, and when and why, and whether anyone—even once—has told the truth, is impossible to know. Even perhaps, in some ways, for the tellers.

These are kids (teenagers, child-adults—it's hard to know what to call them) for whom truth, as a value, is as weightless as air on the moon. Like love, hope, goodness, friendship, the future: an abstraction, without meaning or place in their world. They could name not a soul, not one, who has ever earned a nickel, escaped the streets, or bought an extra hour of life because of truth. Or lived poorer or died sooner because of its lack. To ask them to honor it, or to renounce falsehood, or to feel guilt when they don't, is to ask them to find beauty in a poem about a purple sunset they've perhaps seen once in a book.

Some few things are known for sure. Christian Prince had been at a party that night, at the Aurelian Senior Society in Yale's Strathcona Hall. It had ended at 1:00 A.M. There had been some talk then, among friends at the door, of going for pizza at Naples, a block or two away. Christian declined. He had lacrosse practice in the morning.

His friends left him at the steps of Strathcona, heading south for their pizza and beer. He walked a block east on Grove Street, then north on Hillhouse Avenue. His off-campus apartment, above a running-shoe store at the corner of Whitney and Trumbull, was four or five minutes away.

He made it halfway there. A Yale graduate student, James van Bergen, driving north with friends on Hillhouse, was the first to spot the body. He parked and got out. It was 1:15 or a minute or two after. Almost no time had passed.

"We were headed up the hill, it was totally deserted . . . a very clear, cold night. There were a lot of stars, the wind was blowing. It was not a good night to be outside. . . .

"In front of Saint Mary's Church, directly in front of the church's middle set of stairs and right in the middle of the sidewalk, was a young man, spread-eagled on his back, with his head turned toward Grove Street and his feet toward Trumbull. . . . His legs were several feet apart, his arms were out to his sides. . . . He was lying exactly in the middle between the street and the church, as if he'd come tumbling down the stairs and landed right there. . . .

"I yelled. There was no response. His mouth was slightly open, his eyes were glazing over."

There was a spot of blood on Christian's trousers, some abrasions above his left eye, and a small bullet hole in the lapel of his overcoat, which had belonged to his father. His wallet was found—its forty-six dollars, credit cards, and hockey stubs still intact—across Hillhouse Avenue, more than a hundred feet away.

The ambulance arrived at the trauma center of Yale–New Haven Hospital at 1:43 A.M. There were no discernible vital signs. A team of four doctors opened the chest to reach the heart, which by then had emptied of blood. For twenty-three minutes, new blood was infused through IVs, drugs were given, electroshock performed. There was no response. At 2:06, the patient was declared dead.

His family buried him three days later, each of the four Princes laying a single red rose on the coffin before it was lowered belowground.

In the church, the overflow of mourners filled chairs along both walls. Twenty-year-old Yale athletes held hands and cried openly. Ted Senior read from Plato ("The hour of departure has arrived . . ."), Ted Junior from the Psalms. A schoolteacher, as lovingly as a parent, spoke of the dead boy's "simple habit of always doing what was right. . . ."

Sister Jackie, ramblingly, back and forth between giggles and tears, addressed her words to the coffin in the aisle: of omelettes and overnights, old girlfriends, silly secrets, cooking lessons gone awry. The church laughed with her, but nervously and never for long.

"It's hard to lose your baby brother and hard to lose one of your best friends. To lose both at once is almost too hard to bear. So I'm going to keep calling on you, Christian.

"I don't want to end talking, Christian, because it makes it all seem real. . . ."

At Yale, the flags flew at half-mast. Outside Saint Mary's Church, a vigil of mourners lit candles in the rain and prayed. The *New York Times* ran two stories, both with pictures, in as many days: "At Yale, Fear and Anger Join Grief Over Slaying." Local papers sought out students for reaction: "It is tragic. Everyone is stunned that something like this could happen to one of us," a sophomore told the *New Haven Register.*

More than a thousand letters, written in the months that followed, today fill shoebox after shoebox in the basement of the Prince family home. The eulogies, some in writing, others now preserved on tape, were too many to count or recall: from family, friends and teammates, schoolteachers, a minister, a coach, a United States senator.

There were songs sung, prayers offered, poems recited, cassettes taped, stories and columns from newsrooms in four states. The president's wife sent her sympathies: "For the loss of your precious Christian . . ."

Christian Prince was New Haven's sixth murder victim of 1991. Its fifth, Joseph Ford, shot to death a day earlier, was fifteen, black, and poor. He was mourned by family and friends that Sunday, in a vacant lot a block from where he died.

Ten days later, in the early morning of February 27, seven members of the New Haven Police Department tracked a blue Honda to an apartment on Winchester Avenue, across the street from the Oasis Lounge. They found a cache of guns— revolvers, semiautomatics, a shotgun—but nothing that could be matched, with any certainty, to the bullet in Christian Prince's chest. By ten weeks later, there were still no leads in the case.

Randy Fleming was in the gun-house that morning the police came—along with Andre Edwards, also known as "G-Man," a homeless thirteen-year-old drug addict with nowhere else to go, and Drew ("Jamaican Drew") Fairweather, then seventeen, surrogate father to G-Man and keeper of the guns. The two older boys were charged and released. G-Man, a child by any measure, would spend much of the next two years in and out of detox centers.

On May 10, a Friday, Randy Fleming was arrested again, this time on the street for possession of marijuana. He was taken to the Union Street police station. Over the next three hours, in the custody of two detectives, he was read his rights, given a pack of cigarettes, then taken to McDonald's for lunch.

Between times, he answered questions. What might have moved him to answer them, what he may have asked in return, and how much or little the police already knew, will almost certainly never be told. But by the end of that afternoon, the Prince murder case had itself a witness. Six days later, officially, it was in the hands of the courts.

Question: Okay, I want to ask you some questions about a murder that happened, on February 17, 1991. Are you willing to answer my questions at this time?
Answer: Yes.
Q: How do you know about the murder?
A: I was there.
Q: Okay, and you were there with—?
A: Duncan, Thumbhead, Rob and me.

It went from there. Thirty-one pages in transcript, at intervals over nearly two hours, broken in the middle for a trip
through the city to reenact the crime:

We seen him walkin' toward us—that guy, the Yalie.
So then we came down the street, and we made a
U-turn and we parked. . . . Then he says, "I'm gonna
stick that nigger up right there, I'm gonna stick that
nigger up right there."
Then he jumped out the door, pulled his mask
down and ran toward him. And then he pulled the gun
out and said, "gimme your money, gimme your
money. . . ."
"Here, take the money"—[the victim] said, "here,
take the money." . . . He went like this—yes, he
went like this—he handed him the wallet. . . .
I seen him holdin' the pistol point-blank at his face,
then I seen him go wavin' his arm. I seen him wave the
gun, I seen him go like that to his face. . . .
He was lookin' at the car down the street, goin', "I
should shoot this cracker, I should shoot this cracker."
Then I just heard it go POW! POW! POW!—five times.
. . . He fell sidewards. . . .
Then I seen Dunc runnin' back to the car—and then
he said, "I dropped the wallet, I dropped the wallet." . . .
I axed him why. I said, "Why'd you shoot him?
Why'd you shoot him? You had a wallet, so why'd you
shoot him?" . . . He started sweatin' and swervin' the
car, and then I said, "Man, take me back to Winchester, man, take me back, don't got nothin' to do with it,
man, my name ain't in it, man. . . ."

He was goin'—man, he wasn't like sayin' nothin',
man. Then when we got to the house, he was goin', like
—"I didn't do it, man, I didn't do it, I didn't do it,
man." . . . He was tryin' to deny it to me and I was
there. You know what I'm sayin'? . . .

Everything you need to know is there, man.

Dunc Fleming was arrested the following Thursday, May 16,
at his home on Winchester Avenue. He was charged with robbery and felony murder, then held pending trial at the New
Haven city jail. He was sixteen. Bail was set at a million dollars.

He is nineteen today and has been tried twice for those
crimes. And still, he says, he was nowhere near Hillhouse
Avenue that night. "Can't be two places at one time. You tell
me, man, how'm I gonna be that?"

But he's found some comfort, he claims, in the isolation of
his days in jail. "I'm here, I figure, for one reason. It's 'cause
Somebody Else"—and here he points with his thumb to the
visitors'-room ceiling above us—" 'cause Somebody Else, He
be wantin' me here. . . . Lotta people from 'round my way
been gettin' killed these past four, five years. He just savin' me
from somethin' worse, lookin' out for me. That's how I figure
it."

So you believe in God? I ask. As much as anyone else,
Dunc says. And forgiveness? Yes, he says, he believes in that,
too: "People are people, we all mess up sometime. . . ."

What about Randy Fleming? I want to know. He put you
here. How does forgiveness apply to him?

He doesn't answer, then does. But his answer is more parable than response.

"What goes 'round comes 'round. Now, say you was to shoot me, man—shoot me *bad*—and I was walkin' with this shitbag tied 'round me, or paralyzed or somethin'—and you be runnin' 'round laughin', saying, 'I got that guy, he'll never walk again.'

"Well, I'm gonna want to get you—couldn't be no other way. . . ."

11

Both trials took place, nine months apart, at the county Superior Court in downtown New Haven. At the first, in late May of 1992, Dunc Fleming was charged on four counts: two of murder—one with intent, the other not; one of conspiracy to commit robbery ("a corrupt agreement to do an unlawful act"); and the fourth of attempted robbery. Convictions on any three would put him in jail for most of the rest of his life. None carried a penalty of less than six years.

The first trial lasted a week. The jurors were out three days, then returned with mixed verdicts: guilty of conspiracy, not guilty of murder with intent. On the final two charges—felony murder and attempted robbery—the jury had deadlocked. It was said that the vote had been seven-to-five for acquittal, though this was never confirmed.

On the conspiracy charge, Dunc was sentenced to nine years and sent to the Cheshire correctional center, where I would meet him for the first time four months later.

The state, at that point, had the option of dropping the case. It chose not to. The retrial, on the remaining two counts—carrying a combined penalty of up to forty years—was convened nine months later, the first week of March 1993.

12

Ted Prince and James Fleming, Srs., leaving aside the obvious differences, look a lot alike. Both have strong jaws in wide, oval faces, high foreheads, and deep-set eyes. Ted Prince, by nearly half a foot, is the taller of the two, though both are large, slope shouldered, and round through the middle. Jim Fleming is younger by six years—he is fifty—though if you saw the two together you might take him for the older man.

One walks briskly, in long strides. The other's walk is pained and halting, on crutches he has only just learned to use. Both men smile easily. But there is a vacantness to the smiles, oddly the same, that suggests an act of will. It does not take long to see, with either man, the pain behind the veil.

The two fathers, over more than sixty hours of tedium, burlesque, and simple grotesqueness—wall maps, endless arguments, broken witnesses, gory photos, bloody clothes —were never more than twenty feet apart. They sat, through two trials in nine months, like guests at a church wedding— Jim Fleming next to his son or his wife, Ted Prince with his children, then alone—on their respective sides of the court- room aisle. They never spoke, or shook hands, or—so far as I know—even nodded hello. Once, I think, they shared an elevator; another time, as I watched, they passed within inches in a crowded space. Yet for all that proximity, and all the commonness that linked them—pain, loss, dignity, a father's love—they parted at the end the same strangers they had come.

Through the week of Dunc's first trial, in May 1992, Jim Fleming sat with his son: the two of them, in suit and tie, shoulder to shoulder at the defense table. By the time of the retrial, Dunc had turned eighteen: an adult now by the state's standards, allowed only his lawyer for company. So his father sat in the gallery, on the defendant's side of the court, between his crutches and his wife.

Other than that—and some witnesses who "disappeared" in the months between trials—the two versions had little to mark them apart. Both hung on the avowals of the same parade of teenage felons, who lied under oath without shame. Neither produced much real evidence: fingerprints, a motive, a gun that matched a bullet, a witness who could be believed. In neither one did Dunc Fleming take the stand. He sat through both, expressionless, eyes drifting, as "experts" droned on about chest wounds and shell casings, and his fellow 'Ville Boys, dull eyed and monotoned, tripped over stories that changed as they spoke.

■ ■ ■

Randy Fleming's eyewitness statement, a year old already by
the time the first trial opened, was the heart of the case against
Dunc. Everything else hung around it, as trimming or disproof:
the caliber of the "death bullet," the angle of a pistol-whip, the
location of the wallet, the color and make of the car. Without
Randy's statement, there was no case at all. With it, there was
a plotline that could be fleshed out or stripped bare—depending on whose lies weighed heavier.

He was called to the stand, for the first time, the second day
of the opening trial. At the first question, he pleaded the Fifth
Amendment. The jury was dismissed. The judge and lawyers
huddled briefly, and a decision was reached: He would be
given immunity, could not be tried for any role in the crime. In
exchange, he would have to testify.

But immunity wasn't the problem. Randy Fleming, it
seemed now, was scared. To stand by his statement in court—
he had told a detective, as it turned out, months before—could
cost him his life on the street. True or not, it didn't matter.
There was no immunity for a rat.

And so, caught between unfriendly worlds, he did the only
thing he could: "I said it but it ain't true. . . . They pressured
me—they'd give me so much time I wouldn't believe it, they
gonna hit me with felony murder and conspiracy and all that
junk. . . . They forced me. I couldn't see my mother, I had
no lawyer, what could I do?"

The state's attorney, Mike Dearington, square jawed and
silver haired—a near ringer for Jack Kemp—did his best with
what he had. Weren't you read your rights? he asked the witness. Sworn to the truth? Bought lunch? Treated fairly? Didn't
you initial every page?

"They forced me, man. . . . You tryin' to confuse me, man.

You don't got no evidence. I don't know why you keep askin'
the same questions over and over, man. I don't know nothin'. I
wasn't there, man. I can't help you, man. . . ."

What about the photos he'd identified: of "Rob-base,"
"Thumbhead," and Duncan, the three boys he'd said were with
him in the car that night?

"They had pictures lined up—four niggers, man. . . .
What is this, a racial thing?"

It descended into farce. Dearington asked that the tape of
Randy's statement, now sworn to be a lie, be played aloud for
the jury. The defense objected. The judge allowed the tape.
For the thirty-five minutes it took to play through, Randy
Fleming sat hunched on the stand, muttering and shaking his
head.

Not long after, it was G-Man's turn. Fourteen by now—
looking not a day over twelve, on loan from a detox center—he
told the story of a gun: Dunc had borrowed it—"to do some
stickups," G-Man guessed. He'd returned it two hours later.
He'd returned it two *days* later. He'd wrapped it in a shirt,
poked it with a pipe—"to make the barrel bigger"—before it
was finally left on a shelf. All this had occurred in a sequence
that could exist only in a dream.

Frank Iannotti, Dunc's court-appointed lawyer, a rumpled,
jug-eared Italian with the tenacity of a mastiff, lit into G-Man
with raised voice, curled lip, and a tone brittle with disgust.
Any fourteen-year-old I know would have left the stand in
tears:

"Oh, you're marvelous. You were asleep in that apartment at
ten o'clock, yet at 11:30 you were on Huntington Avenue—but
you got in the car with him at nine o'clock and didn't return
until after you'd *'chilled'* for about two hours? Would you look
at the people of the jury and explain that to them, please, Mr.
Edwards?"

Sheepish, a little glazed, but not a bit daunted: "I mighta got the times mixed up."

Through both trials, there were moments like these. Times of low farce and comic sadness, of children being savaged so badly you wanted to look away. The lies were so bold they seemed innocent, the truths so sad you grew wistful for the lies. That it all took place in a courtroom—black robes, oak panels, the weightiness of truth and right—made it feel sometimes that it could not, possibly, be happening at all.

G-Man, at the second trial—bushy haired, in a blue windbreaker, arriving and departing in that shuffle that belongs only to kids—was asked about Drew, the keeper of the guns, with whom he'd lived until the police shut down their home.

"He took care of me," he said. Like a father? he was asked. He nodded, and seemed to smile. They'd "smoked weed" together sometimes; they'd "hung out on the Av." He was as proud as any boy you've ever seen.

Drew, like G-Man, was a witness at both trials. He chewed gum, spoke in sentences that trailed off at the ends, and glared back at his questioner from eyes that were slits in his head. He was thin and rangy, with a fuzz haircut and a shirt that seemed glued to his chest.

He made no mention of G-Man. He spoke, mostly, of the house they'd shared together—the "arsenal," as it had come to be called—and of the weapons he'd loaned out for cash. Yes, he said, he'd loaned one to Dunc: a .22 revolver, "a couple of days" before Christian Prince had died. He hadn't asked the purpose. He figured it was for a stickup—"or maybe somebody botherin' him." He spoke as you might speak of the extra tickets you had to a concert or ball game.

"When somebody borrow a gun from me, it's either to rob

somebody or they got a problem with somebody. I don't care
what the purpose is—if they're a friend, I give it to 'em."

The final seconds of Christian Prince's life were reprised—at
both trials—by an expert on such things: a thin-lipped Russian graybeard named Arkady Katznelson with a heavy accent
and eight thousand autopsies behind him. What might have
happened, what hadn't happened, what had happened for sure
—a dead body, for this man, held no secrets.

The victim, he said, had been struck in the face with a
"blunt object," probably a gun or a fist. He hadn't resisted—
there were no "defensive wounds." He had fallen, not sideways as Randy Fleming had claimed, but backward onto
his head.

The bullet wound—"half an inch to the left of the midline,
through the periocartal sac, the right side of the heart and
lower lobe of the right lung"—may not have killed him right
away. He could have "walked, even run," for several seconds,
possibly a minute or more.

Could he have been shot near the spot his wallet was found
—as Randy Fleming had claimed—then made it across Hillhouse to die by the steps of the church?

"Yes," said the Russian. "It is possible . . . He had well
developed musculature. He was a young, muscular man."

There were photos: black and white, of Christian's nude
upper body, a small, clean hole where the bullet had entered,
two more—one by each collarbone—from which catheters had
pumped blood and fluid into the heart, and a final hole, larger
and not so clean, into which a chest tube had been inserted to
decompress the blood. They were passed to the jurors, who
passed them—wincing openly—among themselves.

■ ■ ■

Ted Prince, through the first three days of the second trial, sat calm but riveted. He never, that I saw, left the courtroom for a minute, or took his eyes off a witness, or seemed less than fully there. I began to feel in watching him—and in talking with him when the court took its breaks—that Christian for him was somehow *in* that room, and that to miss a word or a moment would be to break faith with his son.

Then, on the afternoon of the third day, Arkady Katznelson took the stand. And Ted Prince closed his eyes. For most of the next forty minutes, as his son's murder was relived through the clues of bruises and blood, he did not open them once. He sat rigid: head bowed, body slightly forward, one hand gripping the back of the seat in front of him. His eyes were squeezed shut. The knuckles of his hand, at moments, were white. But his face was as blank as a stone. I couldn't know if he was praying, or dying inside, or both.

Later that afternoon, after court had recessed, he went alone in a cold rain to a field behind Yale Bowl, to watch in silence as his son's old lacrosse mates ran through preseason drills in the mud. But practice was cancelled almost before it began, so he went to the locker room instead.

You think they got four people to *lie?*" Mike Dearington asked the jury—as bitingly as he could manage, for he's not the biting type—in his summation at the close of the retrial. "You really believe that? You really believe the system is that *corrupt?*"

Randy Fleming, he said, had told the truth two years before. G-Man and Drew, in essence at least, had told the same truth now. The stories had too much in common, too many small

threads—"the small things, the little things"—to have been
invented or coerced. As for their differences—"some inconsis-
tencies, a few denials"—all they proved, he said, was that
there'd been no rehearsing done.

"Variations lend truth" was how he put it. It was a creative
notion—building strength from weakness, a single "common
thread" from the ramblings of teenage boys. But to believe
otherwise, he told the jurors—to believe what he called
"the frame-up argument"—was "to insult everyone in this
court."

He made short work of Randy's recanting—as he'd done,
with a kind of homespun eloquence, nine months before.

"It reminds me—and I'm probably dating myself—but as a
child there used to be this little bird you put in a full glass of
water, and the head went up and down. . . . It reminded me
of Mr. Fleming on cross-examination, the head going up and
down—just answering 'yes-yes-yes' to all those questions.
. . . 'So the police forced you to do that? They made you do
that?' . . . 'Yes-yes-yes'—Do you *believe* that? . . .

"Is there any doubt in your mind that Duncan Fleming
shot Christian Prince, unmercifully shot him without any reason, a cold-blooded murder—then bolted out of there and
headed back to Winchester Avenue? Is there any doubt
at all?"

Frank Iannotti is in his glory at summations. They were made
for him. He is an actor. He shouts and bullies and rants and
prances, flails his arms with every new point, uses clerks as
props to act out muggings—even when he *isn't* summing up.
Rules and strictures don't suit him. The courtroom, through the
first nine-tenths of a trial, seems far too small a stage.

"Where are the *GUNS?* Where is the *CAR?*" The words were whip-cracks. He stood, bug-eyed, neck craned and swiveling like a turtle's, letting the questions sink in. The jury seemed in awe.

"They've got no leads, no arrests, no name—so what do they do? They start pulling *KIDS* off the street. . . . *KIDS,* they found *KIDS!* All they can do is shake down some *BLACK* kids. . . . 'Don't worry,' they say, 'we'll get a name.' . . ."

He dismissed Dunc's accusers—as he'd done at the first trial—with a mix of pity and contempt. G-Man's words to the court, he said, were "the unfortunate testimony of a stoned-out, poor, pathetic fourteen-year-old drug addict." As for Randy Fleming's first statement: "A young man under arrest for drugs, being questioned for a murder. . . . He was just saying words."

Then, abruptly, he stopped—and froze, a yard from the jury box. For five or six seconds, you could hear breathing in the court. Finally, he turned and walked—slowly now, head down, as though suddenly lost in thought—back to the defense table, where he stopped behind his client's chair.

Almost tenderly, he placed a hand on Dunc's shoulder. His voice now was as soft as a girl's.

"An inner-city black kid, probably won't do anything with his life anyway. He wasn't going to go to Yale, probably wasn't going to go to college. . . .

" 'Let's get a conviction,' they say. 'In twenty-four hours we'll forget about it. . . .' "

He was ready for his closer. Mike Dearington would object to it, would say it was irrelevant, that it was going too far—and the judge would agree and order it stopped—but by that time the seed had been laid:

"You have to *live* with yourselves," Frank Iannotti told the jury now, scanning its faces as though they, not Dunc, were on trial. "You have to look in the mirror every day . . .

"Can you say you're *sure* [Dunc Fleming] is guilty?"—and here he stooped forward, a foot from the nearest juror, a middle-aged white woman with short graying hair, who shifted, scratched her head, and tried to look away. His eyes were on a perfect plane with hers.

"Are you *sure?*" he asked again. She met his eyes. He held them for a second, then moved to those at her left: "Are you *sure?*" he asked again.

And so it went, on down the line, through the first row of jurors and half of the next: "Are you *sure?* . . . Are you *sure?* . . . Are you *sure?*"

The jury began deliberations at a little after three in the afternoon on Monday, the eighth of March. Two hours later they went home for the day.

Dunc Fleming spent that night, and the one that followed, in a holding cell in the New Haven city jail. His days would be spent in the courthouse basement, to be close at hand when a verdict was announced. Ted Prince, the trial now ended, flew home on an afternoon plane. Jim Fleming, who'd been coughing badly all day, collapsed in a car in front of the courthouse. He was helped out of it by the driver, who held him erect while he reeled and gasped for breath. The gasping passed, and he was driven home. Once there, he said his prayers, ate what little would stay down, and tried his best to sleep.

Tuesday morning a juror phoned in sick. The other eleven, at the courthouse already, were told to go home and come back the next day. In the hallways, among the reporters and trial

The Prince family, about
1977. *From bottom left:*
Jackie, Sally, Ted Sr.,
Ted Jr., Christian.

left: Summer 1977. New London,
New Hamphire. Christian is
at right.

below: The Prince family at Jackie's
graduation from Yale

right: Christian in Vermont, two weeks before his death

below: Christian as a freshman on the Yale lacrosse team

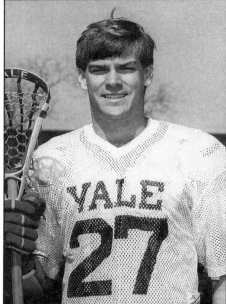

below: The Prince family in New Hampshire, summer of 1990. Christian is second from left

Julia Fleming and Duncan in late 1975

above: Jim Fleming and Duncan at King's Dominion, 1982

right: Duncan break dancing at Disney World in 1981

left: Duncan on the porch of the Fleming home at Easter, 1984 or 1985

below: Jim and Julia Fleming, New Year's Eve, 1990

Duncan as a teenager, a self-taken photo collage

watchers who had stayed with the case, there was talk now that the verdict might not come before the weekend.

On Wednesday morning at ten-thirty the jury went back into session. As before, Jim Fleming was there. He would stand, for most of the rest of the day, on his crutches in the hall outside the courtroom, leaning backward against a wall. From time to time, his wife brought him sodas or crackers from the little cafeteria downstairs.

More than once, he was offered a chair. Each time he declined. A week's worth of sitting, the doctor had told him, had caused a buildup of fluid in his lungs—"from the diabetes, y'know, the heart don't pump it out so good no more."

He had pills, he said, to help keep his lungs clear, but he hadn't been taking them lately. "It makes me have to go to the bathroom all the time, y'know, and I was afraid that the judge, y'know, if he see me comin' and goin' from the room—well, he might just say somethin' to me, y'know, and I didn't want that. Didn't want *nothin'* like that."

The wait was less than five hours. At a few minutes after three in the afternoon, word came from the jury room—a verdict had been reached. Reporters rushed to phones to tell editors to hold space; both lawyers appeared from nowhere. Dunc was brought up from the basement. The court was reconvened.

Jim Fleming looked deathly sick. Shakily, a step at a time, with his wife at his side, he made his way into the courtroom, where he took his seat just inside the door—then began to shake and sweat. Watching him over my shoulder from the row in front, I felt sure he was going to collapse. Instead, suddenly, with a strength it didn't seem he had, he raised himself on his crutches, mounted them, and hobbled weakly, alone, from the room.

"My stomach was in knots—bigger'n my fist, it seemed like. My legs was shakin'; I couldn't get my breath. I said to my wife, 'Babe,' I said, 'I can't make it, y'hear, I'm too scared and nervous. I got to get out.' "

They filed in singly: nine whites, three blacks, two women for every man. Their faces sent no sign.

Dunc was led in by a bailiff and took his seat next to Frank Iannotti. Seconds later, abruptly—in a gesture probably no one in the courtroom missed—he swiveled in his chair and looked backward over his shoulder to the seats to the left of the door. Only his mother returned his look. His brow knotted briefly. He turned back slowly and faced the front.

"The defendant will please rise and face the foreman."

He stood, hands clasped in front of him, and met the eyes of a white-skinned, white-haired, gentle-looking man in his fifties in suit and tie. The man stood also, and looked back. For the ten or twelve seconds it took, neither boy nor man took his eyes from the other's.

"Not guilty."

And then the second count: "Not guilty" again.

Julia Fleming, in the row behind me, sobbed without control, ignoring the tears that rolled off her face to her breast. Other than that, there was no sound in the courtroom. Dunc remained standing, expressionless, hands still clasped in front of him, until the time for standing had passed. Then, in a single, fluid motion that abandoned manliness for the drained terrors of a boy, he turned, eyes closed, and threw his arms around Frank Iannotti, who—unembarrassed—hugged him fiercely back.

Jim Fleming, in the hall outside, still unknowing, still gasping for breath, was reached by his wife:

"My baby's comin' home, my baby's comin' home," she said, and threw her arms around his neck. He sagged on his crutches like a tree limb under snow, pulled her briefly but tightly to his chest, then made his way to a corner, where he wept silently alone.

13

All around Jim Fleming, in the North Carolina of his youth, there were family dying.

His sisters first. The oldest one, years before he was born: a fall into a tub of scalding wash water, at the age of six, in the family's backyard—"There was nothing nobody could do." Then the second, dead at birth four years later.

Then his father, James Henry Brockett, for whom young Jim was named: dead of a "ruptured ulcer" at forty-eight, less than a year after the birth of his son. Jim might never have known the man anyway, even had he lived: He was married to another woman, by whom he'd had four kids. But at least, says his son today, "I would have had a poppa I could have said was mine."

Then his grandfather, who was more like a father really: Herbert Fleming, who owned a gas station and general store on the main street of a little town called Ayden (population four thousand or so). "A businessman, that's what he was," his grandson says today. "I loved him. I looked up to him. I looked up to what he did."

Young Jim spent his third-grade year in Ayden, living on his grandfather's farm. The two grew close. A year later, Herbert Fleming was dead.

Which left his mother: Sophie Fleming, the oldest of Herbert's ten kids. She'd been married years before, in the twenties, to a man named John Brown. But they'd split up—"after not too many years" is Jim's best guess today—and she took back her name.

Sophie was close to forty by the time young Jim was born, in the summer of 1943. Of the three other children she'd had already—one more by Brockett, two by Brown—two were dead by then; the third, a half brother nearly twenty years Jim's senior, had "run his age up and joined the army."

And so, for the first seventeen years of her youngest child's life, it was just the two of them.

They lived in three rooms at the corner of a house at 1115B Clark Street in Greenville, fifteen miles northwest of Herbert's old place. Jim went to school at South Greenville Elementary, to meeting and Sunday school—"every Sunday morning from the time I could walk"—at the Baptist church across town. Sophie meanwhile, who'd left school pregnant before she'd learned to read, cooked meals and polished silver for some of the white folks in town.

"It was a hard life for her, bein' a cleanin' lady all those years—but the peoples she used to work for, they'd take care of her sometimes. . . .

"They used to buy things for her to give to me, y'know—Christmas presents, stuff like that. Bought me a bike one time, so I'd have one, y'know, like the other kids in town. They was good people. Same family, fifteen years—the Ross family. Then the Blount family after that. Good people. They took care of us."

Sophie Fleming worked sixty years in and around Greenville —until she had a stroke not long ago at the age of eighty-five. She was caretaker, at the time, to a ninety-year-old woman. She is ninety herself today, and still there.

"I wake up some mornings with her on my mind? Well, I just jump right on that phone and start to talkin'—'How you bein', Mama?' Once, twice a week at least I call her, sometimes more than that," Jim says.

At seventeen, young Jim went north to Philadelphia, to spend a year with his mother's sister, Blanche Simmons, in her neighborhood row house on Parrish Street. The following June, 1962, he was a member of the graduating class of the William Penn High School.

Then began the jobs. So many of them, a dozen or more, they're a blur in his mind today: a line of drabness stretching across eight years. Why he took the first one—or even what it was—or how the first became the second or the third, or why he never looked for anything better—all that has been lost to time.

"There was never no money, never no time to look" is all he can say today. He seems confused by the question.

Washing pots in the kitchen of a New Jersey boys' school.

Scraping the excess food from plates at a Chinese restaurant in Philadelphia's downtown (thirty-five cents an hour, seventy-two hours a week, "you had to work the seventy-two hours before they'd pay you a dime"). Two years as a janitor at Temple Hospital. Eighteen months unloading trucks for Bluebird Meats.

Somewhere in there, Blanche Simmons died, and Jim was on his own. He moved south then, to Baltimore, where rents were less. He met a girl and moved in with her. He began a new job.

"It was like a golf course, y'know. Only they call 'em country clubs. Hilldale, I think was the name [possibly Hill and Dale, in Phoenix, just outside the city]. I worked in the kitchen, kind of a short-order cook, y'know. It was a pretty good job."

But nothing lasted in those days. He and the girl broke up. "It must have been, I don't know, maybe a year, a year and a half. We had a misunderstanding, I guess you'd say, and I moved out."

And drifted on. Two years at Franklin Hospital—still in Baltimore—where he made beds and swept floors, then a year or so on the assembly line of a "glass company" that may have been a bottling plant. He can't recall what he did there exactly, or how much it paid, only that it had "something to do with making soda bottles."

Drudge jobs. Endless, futureless, mind-numbing jobs that asked nothing of him but his arms and his legs and his time, and paid nothing back but what the law required, sometimes not even that. Thirty-five cents an hour. One dollar, $1.10, $1.50. Sixty, seventy, eighty hours a week. Ten at night till noon the next day, eleven in the morning till three in the morning—six, sometimes seven days at a time. An older man, a weaker man, a man with loftier things on his mind, could never have stood the strain.

"But I was a young man then," he says. "And all I wanted was things of my own."

Julia Smith meanwhile had grown up on West Twelfth Street in Greenville—the corner of Twelfth and Clark. Most of the view out the Smiths' front door was of the rear of Sophie and Jim's little home. Julia's memories of the neighbor boy—impish, irreverent, a crack marble shooter with a passion for dancing—go back to three years old:

"We was *kids* together. Hide-and-seek, swingin' in the park, sneakin' out school nights, playin' marbles, all that kinda stuff. We grew up together—went to school together, saw each other near about every day."

Until 1956, when Julia's mother took sick, and the twelve-year-old moved north with her two sisters to live at an uncle's in New Haven: on the first floor of the same three-family walk-up on Winchester Avenue in which, today, thirty-seven years later and one floor higher up, she tends to a gravely ill husband and three (soon to be four) grandchildren whom no father will claim.

She was in New Haven seven years: from sixth grade through twelfth, graduating from Wilbur Cross High School in June of 1963, the same month Jim Fleming landed the job scrubbing pots at the Pennington School for Boys just outside Trenton.

She returned home to Greenville after that, where she would stay nearly four years, picking tobacco and caring for her

mother—until she left for good in early 1967 to
nanny to a Hungarian family just outside New Yor'

But sometime that first summer, the summer of 1965
what both recall as a coincidence of timing), Jim Fleming returned home to Greenville for a visit. The two friends saw each
other—the first time in close to seven years. She was eighteen
now, and had breasts and wore dresses, and was tall and lanky
and moved like a woman. He was nineteen, beefy and strut-
ting, and talked about being a drummer in Bill Black's Combo.
But more than that, he wanted a family, he said.

Neither one will say much about the comings and goings of
those next several years. And what they do say, or most of it, is
fuzzy and piecemeal, or at odds with half of what they've said
before:

There was another woman in Jim's life (at least for a time),
other men in Julia's. He lived in Philadelphia, later in Baltimore, and worked six days a week, sometimes seven. She lived
in Greenville, then in New York. They were never less than
four hundred miles apart. And yet, she will swear to you: "I
took the train to see that man every second weekend for years"
—and he won't dispute it.

What *is* sure: A child was born. Sandra, in early February of
1965. She might have been Jim's or some other man's. How
you figure it depends on how you hear what's said. "I'm not her
real father," Jim says at one point. And at another: "We had
her before we was married. I adopted her after."

Julia says nothing at all, merely shakes her head and looks
away—the signal she gives to let me know that she wants no
part of this.

In the end, at least to hear Jim tell it, it didn't much matter
who the father was. Old Sophie, still living next door in Greenville, filling in as mother for somebody else's child, just got

tired after a while of watching that little girl, four years old by the time Sophie put her piece in, growing up without a father around.

"My mama, she called me one day—she said, 'I think it's time you come home. It's time you come see about your baby.' Well, that's what did it, I swear."

Julia Smith and Jim Fleming were married in Baltimore, in a small ceremony at Jim's niece's apartment, on the seventh of June, 1969. The groom was twenty-five, his bride a year younger.

The future, it must have seemed to both of them, began that day. The drifting, the double shifts, the dead-end jobs, the fatherless little girl with a mother who came and went—ended, all of it, as though it had never been. As though, for Jim Fleming at least, and perhaps for his wife as well, all that had ever really been missing was a reason to try.

Before the year was out, Jim had changed jobs for the last time: from fifteen hours a day at $1.50 an hour as security guard at the Burns Detective Agency, to $2.25 an hour, forty-five hours a week patrolling the aisles of a Reade's (soon to be Rite-Aid) Drug Store in suburban Baltimore—uniformed, badged, and pistoled, a stocky young enforcer with a family to feed and his eye on the ladder up.

Their first home was on Calvert Street: a cramped, boxy, row house apartment for seventy-five dollars a month. They stayed two years, until Sandra reached second grade—then moved to East Baltimore, where the houses, at least, were larger and farther apart. Two years later Tanya was born, then James Duncan a year after that. They moved again, and this time it showed: nine rooms on three floors, where no two children shared a bedroom, a closet for nothing but toys, and room for spreading out.

It was 1976. Jim was working toward his second promotion; Julia was a press operator for London Fog. They had a five-day sitter at twenty dollars a week. Jim belonged to the Masonic Lodge and played poker in the basement game room Friday nights; on Saturdays they went dancing or to ball games. The family album was known as the "Brag Book." The family income, after taxes, was $25,000 a year.

"We went to Atlantic City one time," Jim remembers now, out of nowhere, his voice approaching a lilt. "In the late seventies, right after them casinos came in. Us and this other couple—had dinner in the city first, then drove on down for the night. Those days, I tell you, we had money to blow. . . .

"We went on picnics, out dancing—on weekends we'd just pick up and go. All kinda different things. And concerts too, sometimes.

"Loretta Lynn—remember that one, babe? Loretta Lynn. She's my sweetheart. She can sing for me anytime."

It is sixteen years later, the Tuesday before Thanksgiving of 1992. Jim Fleming will be fifty soon. He has only one leg now, and only one eye that sees. A year from now he will have only one working kidney. He has no money. His daughters are husbandless mothers; his only son is in jail. His muscles have softened and sunken, and the skin on his arms is loose. He is wearing a T-shirt that reads "Sex Is Like Snow. You Never Know How Many Inches or How Long It Will Last."

"Those was good years. The best. We was livin' comfortable, y'know? Everything runnin' smooth and nice—no big crisis or nothin', nobody wantin' for what they don't got."

Tanya's younger child, Takara, a breathlessly beautiful girl of two with dark chocolate skin and eyes like black marbles, is arched face-up across her grandfather's lap, playing with the stubble on his chin. Across the room meanwhile, Julia Fleming is kneeling on the floor, wrestling a shoe onto the foot of her youngest grandchild—eighteen-month-old Terrence—who is giggling and wriggling, trying to make the moment last.

"You know the best thing ever happened to me?" Jim says now absently, as though to the wall or to himself.

"Gettin' married—that's the best thing ever happened in my life. . . .

"Me and Julia, we gonna—what they call that thing they do, babe?"

"Renewin' the vows," his wife answers from the floor, without looking up.

"That's it. We gonna renew the vows—our vows. Soon. 'Ninety-four, ain't that right, babe? The year of our twenty-fifth. Gonna renew them vows—we gonna do it all over again, just like the first time. . . .

"And you know who gonna be the best man?"

He stops now, and smiles broadly. There is a twinkle in his eye. He knows I know what name he will say.

"James, that's who. He gonna be our best man. He gonna give his mama away."

There is an argument about Thanksgiving. It is two days away, and it hasn't been decided yet who will do the cooking— or whether the meal will be turkey or ham.

"I already told 'em," Julia is saying to me, "if my James wasn't gonna be home, I wasn't gonna be doin' no cookin'.

"And so"—and here she turns to Tanya, who is next to me on the couch, staring at the flickerings of the silent TV—"you best get out in the kitchen, girl."

They go back and forth. Who will cook? Turkey or ham? Tanya, after a minute or two of this, loses patience.

"I got other places I can go Thanksgiving."

"Well, you go then. I can cook without you, you know—yes indeed, I can."

Jim has been watching all this, poker-faced, from his chair in the corner. Now, fearing perhaps that I will go away with a clouded sense of the family's togetherness, he turns again to me: "See, how it was when James was home, we used to have a big Thanksgiving. Everybody be here at a certain time, no arguments or nothin'—and we sit down and have dinner in the kitchen. That was the point of Thanksgiving, that was the idea of it all.

"This year, I s'pose, they be givin' him his turkey in the jail. . . ."

"Turkey *nothin'*," Julia half shrieks, disembodied, from the kitchen. "He ain't gonna be eatin' none of their turkey. Only thing that boy like is *chicken*. Chicken, chicken, chicken. His favorite thing in the world is chicken, macaroni and cheese.

"He won't be eatin' none of their turkey—not this Thanksgiving, not *ever*. I seriously doubt that, no sir."

Watching the Fleming family, torn loose from every mooring they had reason to believe was theirs for life, scraping for their dignity under the eyes of a stranger, is like watching a wounded bird, on instinct alone, spinning in circles in its struggle to fly.

Pride in the past. In their marriage vows. In a tradition—broken now—of on-time, argument-free Thanksgivings. In their jailed son's love of his mother's chicken dinners. There is almost nothing else left.

■ ■ ■

What is left is the future. They will leave New Haven, they say. They will go back south where they started, where things were better for them. Once there, they will build a new life.

"This time next year," says Jim, "it be either Baltimore or North Carolina. One or the other, I don't care much which one, but we be *gone* from here. . . ."

But not yet. There are things still that need to be worked out:

"After the holidays, February or March, after we see, y'know, what they gonna do with James. . . . Then I gotta get that new leg they gonna give me, get comfortable movin' around and all—*then* we go lookin' for a house."

They will have Jim's disability money to work with, and possibly Julia's by then ("I'm trying to get on the list, 'cause of my heart and all, but sometimes it takes awhile before they let you know"), and Sandra's and Tanya's welfare checks—providing the grandkids come south with them, which, so far at least, is the plan.

"Tichelle will go, I know that much," says Julia. "And [Tanya's] little one too, I'm pretty sure."

Will that be that okay with Tanya? I want to know.

"It be okay with Tichelle."

I can't help persisting: But Tanya's the legal mother, right?

"Yeah, and I'm the legal *grandmother,* too."

Have the two of them discussed this?

"Nope, no need to discuss it. If I was to ask Tanya, she prob'ly say no. Then she prob'ly say yes."

Jim has been quiet through all this. He chuckles now, softly, and nods his head.

"That's the truth," he says. "That surely is the truth. . . . See, how it is is this—Tanya, she just nineteen years old, and already she got two kids. She don't really know nothin' about what it is to raise kids. She just a baby herself."

The future, for the Flemings, remains what it's been for nearly eight years now, since Jim Senior lost his eyesight, and after that his job—and Julia had her heart attack, and the first of the girls got pregnant.

The future is in free money.

Disability for Jim and Julia. Food stamps. The grandkids' welfare checks. Without free money, there can *be* no future. With it, just possibly, there is a new life down south.

When you're a proud man, as Jim Fleming is, yet must depend on free money for your living, you find new ways of looking at things:

"I know, with my sickness and all, I can't work no more. At least this way, I figure, I won't have to be callin' up nobody, sayin', 'Well, Mr. So-and-So, I won't be able to work today, on account of my bein' sick.' People get tired of that, y'know. They have work that have to be done—and after a while they say, 'Well, I don't need you no more.' And what you gonna do then?"

Jim's disability check, which began six years ago at $611 a month, is a little more than $740 today. Tanya, Sandra, and their three children, according to the formula of the state's welfare board, receive $914 monthly between them. There's another $260 or so in food stamps; medical bills are paid by the state.

The rent on the apartment is $400 a month—which leaves about $1,250 plus the food stamps, to provide for the seven of them (eight before Dunc went to jail). So no one is about to starve—although, as Jim Fleming is fond of saying: "We have to stretch every dime."

(Some, it seems, stretch more than others. The family phone, not long ago, was disconnected when a bill remained unpaid. Tanya's bedroom phone, meanwhile, along with her VCR and cable TV, never missed a beat. When you ask about such things—depending on whom in the family you ask—what you get is a shrug, a stare, or a very small smile. But never a word, never even one.)

The demographers would call them an extended family: three generations, sharing a name, some common resources, and a roof. By some estimates, 40 percent of black America fit this mold.

But what, besides blood, makes a family a family? Love, heritage, honor, security, a unity of cause—the Flemings share none of these. Except perhaps love, which has been so trampled by disappointment over the years it is hard to discern in what passes between them. They are a household of aliens, as disparate as their roots:

Two bitter, sickly, middle-aged adults who grew up poor in the fifties South, whose ethics were shaped more by poverty and plainness than by any sense of the color of their skin; who between them held twelve, fifteen, twenty jobs—as waiter, nanny, janitor, cook, line worker, field worker, washer of pots —whatever it took to put supper on the table and make tomorrow feel less futile than today. They believed in work and God and each other, and the love of their mothers, and the sweetness of music and dance. They were old-fashioned Negroes; even, some would say, Uncle Toms.

And their daughters, and absentee son—raised in the city

on an ethic of sneakers and hate. One pregnant at fourteen, another in jail before he was old enough to vote. They have known more deaths than Christmases; their every dollar comes from the streets or the state. They are modern. Their clothes are leather, and their music is rap. They do not work. I have never seen them smile, except thinly. It is hard to read what, if anything, is in their hearts.

And the little ones, Tichelle, Takara, Terrence (and a fourth one on the way): the fatherless babies. *They*, not the grown ones, are the glue that binds. They are money in the bank: $11,000 a year (with another $1,300 coming) to whoever can claim them, to whoever will give them a roof.

"Without that money," says their grandmother lamely—not knowing, surely, all of what she is saying—"I don't know what we'd do."

"We'd manage," says her husband. But there is only weariness behind his words. "We'd manage, like we always done.

"And anyway, those kids, they not goin' nowhere. The only daddy they ever known is *me.*"

"Well, and I'm their main *mama*, too," Julia says, suddenly feisty now. "That's for sure. Been their main mama since the day they was born."

"Well then, what you got yourself so bothered about?"

"Who said I was bothered? I ain't bothered about nothin'. I'm bothered about the *lottery*—that's what I be botherin' about."

It is as though someone had just reminded Jim Fleming that he'd left a pot on the stove.

"The lottery. Yeah. How much it be now?"

"Seventeen million tonight."

"Seventeen million. That's a lotta money."

"Lotta money is right. I'm gonna get me a *piece* of that

money, too. Goin' down to the store right now, gonna get me a Quik-Pic. Six numbers, let the machine do the pickin'. You don't need but one to win. . . .

"I hit that number, I tell you, I'm *gone*. You better believe it —Atlantic City, the casinos, that's where you find *me*. Either there or Vegas, one . . ."

Her husband shakes his head. Slowly, rhythmically, as far to each side as his neck will allow. He is smiling slightly through pursed lips, and his eyes are lowered to his lap. When he speaks, it is as though he were addressing the floor.

"Not me, no sir. I win, first thing I do is buy us a house— someplace far away from here. Next thing is, I get my son outta jail. I take that money and I go get me a lawyer, that's what. . . .

"They say, 'A lawyer's gonna cost you five thousand dollars'? I say, 'No problem, mister, here's your five thousand dollars, here's whatever you want—now you just get my boy outta jail.'

" 'Cause that's all it is—it's a game, is all. It's all about money, and whoever's got it wins."

Julia leaves while we are talking. She returns not long after with milk, diapers, and five Quik-Pic tickets. Five days later, the family's phone is shut off.

But in Jim Fleming's mind's eye, where pride has outlived its sources and phone bills don't intrude, there is still that house that the lottery will buy: on a broad piece of North Carolina flatland somewhere near where old Herbert used to live, big enough for the eight of them, with shutters and gables and room to run around. James is there, of course (he is just James now, no more "Dunc," no more need of street names), freed by the lawyers who can free anyone with five thousand dollars to spend; and his two big sisters and their baby girls and boy. The sunshine is unimpeded by rooftops, the nights unbroken by shots, and old Sophie lives just down the road. There is a poker table in the basement and a Winnebago parked outside.

"Seventeen million," he says again as his wife is on her way out the door. And again: "Seventeen million"—but it is more a whisper now. He is still smiling though, and still staring at his lap—as though to look up would be to break the spell:

"I could sure set a lotta things right with seventeen million."

14

It is an evening in late April 1993, twenty-six months since Ted and Sally Prince have lost their son. They are sitting, over a midweek supper of salad and spaghetti and white wine, at opposite ends of their kitchen table. I am between them on one side, daughter Jackie on the other.

"I feel sometimes that I ought to apologize to Ted," Sally is saying to me now—but her eyes shift in midsentence to her husband's—"for him not having a happy wife."

Ted Prince looks across at her, his eyes soft and grateful, but says nothing in return.

"I'm sorry, Ted. I know I've been miserable, I know it's been hard for you, but"—and here her voice catches and her eyes fill with tears—"but the pain just *never* ends. Never . . .

"I guess in some way I don't want it to end—that would be

the first step toward forgetting him, and I could never do that, not as long as I live. . . .

"Oh God, sometimes I think all I want to do is just *die*—just to see him again, to be with him again."

In her husband's answer, tender and slow worded, and edged with the sadness that they share, there is no trace of alarm. It is clear he has grown accustomed to his role.

"The way I see it, if I'm going to be with him again, then that's going to last forever. Forever, Sally, an eternity. And whatever time I've got remaining is so little in comparison that I may as well enjoy the two I still have left.

"And if I'm *not* going to see him—well then, I've still got to get the most out of the others in the meantime. Either way, I guess what I'm saying is, life goes on."

Sally Prince looks at me now—searchingly, as though for some assurance I couldn't possibly give. "You see how *different* we are? I try to think of it the way he does—I keep telling myself, 'I have two children, a wonderful husband'—but it's not enough, it's never enough. Because in the end—in the end it really doesn't matter to me if I live or die."

"Well, I'd say that's an *improvement*," Ted Prince answers. But there is a small smile on his face and no unkindness in his tone.

A minute later, his plate empty, he rises from the table and walks quietly from the room, leaving the three of us to our talk and what remains of our wine. He will not be back. The Washington Capitals are facing elimination in the Stanley Cup playoffs. The game is an hour old already, and Ted Prince is a fan.

There was a reception at the Prince family home the afternoon of the day Christian was buried. No one who was there seems able to forget it.

"An orgy of grief," a family friend remembers. "Twisted, eerie, with this strange sense of numbness. I left shaking."

They all tell of the same scenes:

Ted Senior, his son's lacrosse stick like some misshapen shepherd's crook an extension of his arm—as though nothing could be more natural than a six-foot, sweat-stained shaft of wood with a basket at the end in the hands of a balding middle-aged man receiving guests in his living room at the funeral of his son—walking absently from room to room, giving and receiving hugs.

His wife, greeting mourners from behind eyes that were glass. "Her face was a death mask," a friend remembers. "Seeing her that day, I realized I'd never before known the magnitude of grief."

And in the corner of one room, like some jerrybuilt battlefield shrine, a crude montage of the dead boy's photos, letters, old school reports. "You weren't sure," says a Yale classmate, "if you were supposed to kneel down or cry."

Larry Downs, a New York psychiatrist and close family friend, was among the guests at the Prince home that day. The pain he witnessed, he recalls, was "unspeakable." It left nothing untouched.

"People in grief sometimes—in the deep, agonizing grief that follows sudden loss—sometimes they just fade away, just literally fade away. They're diminished—their bodies shrink, their shoulders hunch in, they become miniature versions of themselves.

"I've seen it before—in emergency rooms, in Vietnam—but never like that day. The whole family just *shrunk*, just shrunk in front of my eyes. . . .

"Even Ted . . . If you hugged him, he'd come back to life for a minute or two, then start to fade away again. With Jackie the same way, with Ted Junior the same way.

"With Sally, it was worse. If you touched her, you could put life back into her—but it didn't last as long, usually only for just that instant. Then she was gone again. . . .

"Someone five-foot-three shrunk down to five feet—a hug as resuscitation. It was unbelievable, the enormity of it. Awful, awesome. I'll never forget it as long as I live. . . ."

For father, brother, and sister, the healing began that day. For months after, they grieved—they are *still* grieving, each in his or her way. But with every curse uttered or tear shed, their loss becomes more real, more tangible—more a part, however horrible, of the recorded fabric of their days. They have learned the words: "It happened"—murder, injustice, an act of hate, a travesty of everything life was to have led to for a son or brother they will never see again. But it happened. And their lives, however scarred, go on.

Not so for Sally Prince. In the mind of this mother, for whom selfhood and motherhood are hopelessly tied, for a long time after her son had been murdered—he had *not* been murdered. Was not even dead. The world that told her otherwise was mad.

"This event, for Sally—it had simply not happened," says Larry Downs today. "That's the level of denial we're talking about here. Christian was *not* dead. . . .

"Missing maybe—a young child lost in the woods, and you go out and you find him. Or an MIA—a father, a brother, whatever, missing in action—and you sit and you wait for him to come home. But not dead, anything but dead. Death—the finality, the sheer magnitude of death—was too much for this woman's mind to cope with."

I am thinking, as he speaks, of the Sally Prince I'd left that same morning, four or five hours before. We'd shared breakfast —an English muffin, coffee, and juice—at her kitchen table before I'd departed for the airport to catch my plane. Our talk, unlike the night before, had been of gayer things: her daughter's approaching wedding, her husband's passion for sports. There had been, as always, a sadness—she is enveloped in sadness, as though in a cloud—but her smiles had seemed unstrained. She was gracious. We hugged briefly when I left, and wished each other well.

You're talking about madness," I say now to Larry Downs. My mind, in its literalness, is unable to make the jump.

"Not madness. Denial, depression, despair—despair beyond comprehension."

And then he tells me this story: "For a long time after Christian was killed—four months at least, maybe longer— nearly every night at two-thirty or three in the morning, Sally would leave her bed and start prowling—'prowling' is the only word you could use. She'd walk the upstairs hallway, in and out of bedrooms, from one room to the other, looking for her boy. Like a soldier in the jungle on some search-and-destroy mission—figuratively dressed in combat fatigues, bayonet fixed—'You've got my boy, give me back my boy. . . .' "

Sally Prince no longer prowls the halls at night. She can speak of her son today—at least half the time—without giving

in to tears. She smiles now more often than she cries. She is
healing. She has learned the cure of grief.

But none of this changes what Christian's loss has cost her.
Her life, in her own plainest terms, has been destroyed.

"It was wonderful, perfect. I had everything I'd ever
dreamed of—three perfect children, a man I respected and
loved. Nourishing, sharing, a house, a nest, the spiritual side. I
felt so blessed. I thought it would go on forever.

"But that's over now. Poisoned. My life will never be wonderful again."

It is early January 1993, two months before Dunc Fleming's
second trial. We are sitting, facing each other, across the living
room of the family home in Chevy Chase. It is late afternoon,
five o'clock or a little after. The daylight is failing fast.
Through the living room windows that look out on the yard and
patio and the swimming pool beyond, only the trees still hold
their shape.

"I worked hard for what I had. I'm a fighter. I've been a
fighter since I was a little girl. I always believed you got what
you fought for—I know now that's not true. It makes you wonder how there can possibly be a God."

Sally Prince is fifty-four, short and slight—she reaches
barely to her husband's shoulders—with fading blond hair cut
close around her face. She has high cheekbones and dark blue
eyes that narrow when she smiles. Her legs and arms, like
everything about her, are small and tight skinned, and still
with the lines of her youth. She has not lost her prettiness. It
would be hard to take her for older than her years.

For all that, you could not look closely and fail to see that
this is a woman in grievous pain. It shows first in the mouth—
it is hard now, almost cruel looking sometimes, and pulls

tightly at the ends when she smiles. Her eyes from time to time flash uncertainly, as if from sudden fright. She cries often and without warning. Her hands, at odd moments, ball into little fists. It is as though her frame were too small somehow to contain the grief inside.

She is obsessed with death. Near-death stories consume her thoughts and speech: Jackie, as a little girl, her nightgown in flames from contact with a toaster-oven ("If Ted had been at the office, I swear she'd be dead today"); Ted Junior and Christian as teenagers, skidding out of control on an icy road ("Every time I drive past that curve, I think I might have lost them both").

She asks about my own son. Car accidents? Emergency room visits? Have we ever "almost lost him"?

No, I tell her, we've been lucky—"knock on wood."

"Never even a *close call?*" She seems in disbelief.

The subject shifts—it often does—abruptly.

Her older son's hands: "They're so like Christian's, I can't look at them without thinking of him."

She begins, as she so often does, to cry.

I've perhaps never known anyone in rawer pain than Sally Prince. Pain so raw she is helpless, it seems sometimes, even to direct its flow. It spills from her: in fragments, random associations, memories that seem less triggered than simply jarred loose. Her hurt is as naked as a child's. I want to hug her. Instead I ask questions, take notes, and work to meet the sadness of her eyes.

She has lost more, and worse, than a son. She has lost her faith—in life and humanity and the force she calls God. Because of what she paid to earn it, it was the most precious thing she owned. Without it, she says, it is hard for her today to find reasons to live.

For most of us, faith is not so fragile. Or so dearly, or defiantly, prized. It is built slowly, beginning in childhood—like healthy teeth and limbs—from the natural early nurturings that life provides: family, security, religion, the sureness of Santa Claus. By adulthood, if we are lucky, it is part of the fabric that enables our days.

But for Sally Prince, who had few such early blessings, faith was not a process but an act of will. It was built primitively, at first angrily, out of little more than a lonely teenager's need to believe, starting more than forty years ago. The price she paid to earn it, and the terrible cost of its loss, have shaped most of what she is today.

She was born in 1939 in Summit, New Jersey, the daughter of weak, badly matched parents who'd married too young and had neither the love nor the will to make a life for themselves. ("They weren't tough" is how she puts it today.) Her father was a spoiled, directionless sometime-salesman often between jobs. Her mother, a "gentle, very lovely, very loving" young woman who'd married in desperation at nineteen to escape the miseries of her own family's Depression-ruined life, was deep into the bottle before her daughter reached first grade.

"She was a binge drinker. She'd drink for six months, then stop for six months, and everything would be normal again. She'd try so hard to make it up to us, to be the perfect mother. And she was—when she wasn't drinking. She couldn't have been more wonderful.

"Then one day it would be, 'Oh gosh, mother's been drinking again.' It got so she couldn't walk straight, she couldn't talk straight, she'd pass out all the time. I used to think she was going to die.

"But we'd all pretend not to notice; we'd pretend everything was still fine. We were all such play-actors—it makes me so angry now, thinking back."

Sally's father meanwhile kept getting and losing jobs—leaving it to his wife, on the wagon or off, to keep the family afloat. For several years, she ran the bookstore at her daughter's grade school. Before that, she'd worked the day shift at a local hotel.

"She was amazing. She'd come home at five o'clock, start drinking, keep drinking, pass out, then go to work the next morning. She never even had a hangover."

It ended in 1954, the year Sally turned fifteen. It was her mother who left, taking only her bags and her problems, south to Virginia to her own parents' home. Father and daughter, for most of the next two years, lived alone in an old farmhouse on the outskirts of a small New Jersey town—until he took up with Sally's old Sunday school teacher, was home less and less often for supper, and the loneliness grew too heavy to bear.

She went south, at sixteen, to rejoin her mother, who by then had stopped drinking and was getting by as manager of a hospital thrift shop. Her father tried for a while to win her back —threats, bribery, gentle persuasions. When that didn't work, he wrote her out of his life. She never forgave him, though she tried at least once to reconcile. She finds it hard today to speak his name.

She finished school in Virginia, won a scholarship to Sweet Briar, and met Ted Prince in the spring of her junior year. They were married thirteen months later. For the twenty years that followed, her life was a nearly unbroken succession of joys.

. . .

The world is full of unhappy souls who, unwittingly, through blindness or weakness or wounds too deep to heal, rewrite the tired old scripts of mothers or fathers who, themselves, were too weak or wounded to find peace.

Sally Prince is not one of these. She is, as she says, a fighter. Her mother's alcoholism, her father's listless route through life, the failure of both as parents—from as early as her teens, these were the compass points she set her course by, then steered her ship, as though in mutiny, away.

She was not without tools. From her mother, whom she loved dearly despite her weakness, she inherited gentleness and whimsy, and a measure of the grit she would need. From her father she took nothing but her own pain and rage—though these may have been the greatest gifts of all.

"She lived her whole life in this moralistic defiance of her roots," says Larry Downs. "She saw herself as self-made. She had beaten her heritage—it was an enormous part of who she was."

Her pact with life—"It will *not* be that way for me"—in time became its filter: She learned early to scorn weakness and uncertainty, to distrust the college boys who drank too much or seemed rootless or unsure ("I wasn't going to marry a poet"). She took on mantras: "Life is what you make it"; "You're never going to fail." She made As, squirreled away her dollars, and planned to be a teacher.

Through it all—somehow—she stayed pert and pretty, an easy laugher and a generous friend. She dated her share of handsome young men (including at least one poet), smoked and drank at parties, sat up late nights—a philosophy major— debating Nietzsche and Kant. She was a collegian.

But there would be life after college. And Sally Prince's

eyes—always—were on the road ahead. Years before her college days, perhaps as early as the time of her mother's first
drinking binges, she knew precisely what she did and didn't
want.

"I'd battled long enough. I wanted a *life*—to live like I
thought nice people lived. A normal, secure family, a family
without alcoholism, without divorce, without struggles to pay
the bills. I wanted to be *happy*. It didn't seem so much to ask.

"Some people, when they're young, they want to go on to be
doctors or lawyers. . . . I just wanted to have a big family of
towheaded kids."

She got it all—"beyond my wildest dreams, happiness like I'd
never thought possible. I had to pinch myself sometimes."

With each new blessing, her faith took deeper root. And few
of her Sweet Briar classmates could claim to be so blessed: a
law-partner husband with roots in Chevy Chase and Yale,
money enough for every need, three remarkable children, a
marriage as sure and solid as marriages get. Even finally, with
the children nearly grown and time on her hands, a dress-shop
business that started as a hobby and grew, within twelve years,
to eleven stores in three states—"the feeling that you're never
going to fail."

Her faith, so hard won, became unshakable. The core of her
being: that even ghosts can be beaten, that "you get what you
fight for," that life—after all—was kind and just.

"She picked the right husband, had the right marriage,
lived in the right community," says Larry Downs. "Her life was
mapped out. . . .

"And then the children—all wonderful, all winners, all
three at Yale . . .

"They became her banner. She defined herself through them; their successes became hers. They made her—and this is the key—they made her, in her eyes, a *Good Person.*"

Listening to Larry Downs, in his New York office on this late April day, describing the bonding of a mother with her children, I think back to another exchange with Sally, in her living room on that winter evening three months before. She had told me, in summary form, the landmarks of her life: childhood, college years, her marriage to Ted. Except when I asked her to, she'd not lingered on details. A decade might be dispatched in a paragraph or less.

Then she'd come to the births of her children: Jackie in 1962 in Virginia, Ted Junior in 1966, Christian five years after that.

"I've never been able to figure it out," she said, "how all three of them turned out to be so incredible."

But since then? I asked. Since Christian's birth nearly twenty-two years ago—what other milestones?

She smiled at me, warmly but bemused, as though the question had never once crossed her mind—and said exactly this: "That was it, Geoffrey. That was it."

The world is full of Sally Princes," Larry Downs says now. "The kids feeding the parent—it comes down to that. Their successes—with every new one the message is clearer: 'What a wonderful person I am.'

"And the delusion is born. . . . Not only are you good—a good parent, a good person—you can make life what you want it. You're in control of events."

■ ■ ■

And then it happened. Her youngest—"the easiest child, everything he ever did brought us pleasure"—died without reason alone late at night on an empty street while she was with friends on an island off South Carolina—and Sally Prince's faith snapped and shattered like dried bone being crushed underfoot.

"Christian's death, for Sally, was Judgment Day," says Larry Downs. "Literally. A condemnation of her entire existence. It took away the value of her life. If this could have happened [as she saw it], it could only mean one thing—that she was a morally failed human being. . . .

"That's the awful danger of defining yourself through your kids—you live by the sword, you die by the sword. . . ."

Her sanity, for months, hung by what must have seemed a thread. She cried day and night, cut off her family, prowled the halls at three in the morning, talked endlessly about wanting to die. There were delusions: A blond-haired boy from the neighborhood, Larry Downs remembers, at some point *became* her son—an "embodiment," she called him, Christian's spirit refusing to lie down.

Then came the guilt—she blamed herself, she blamed the world, she blamed everything but chance. Then anger, then rage, then hate. She cursed God. She swore revenge. She began talking about getting her hands on a gun.

Even today, two years later, there are still some flashes of this: "I think almost every day about killing him," Sally told me in her living room, "about how I could smuggle a gun in there. But it passes."

■ ■ ■

A bereft mother, torn loose from her moorings, struggling to regain her will to live. A father whose faith and strength and small delights are beacons against the blackness of his family's grief. A son and daughter, unschooled in loss, who jerk heavily —almost daily—between pain and rage.

It could be any family—your family or mine. Comfortable, insulated, unsuspecting, unrolling our tomorrows like carpets down an endless aisle. . . .

And then a sundering: a limb split off, the trunk severed violently, and all the small, easy certainties that make tomorrows of todays are suddenly valueless, gone, as useless as gauze against the cold. We are naked. The personal happens— as it has with Sally Prince. The faces we have fashioned become, inexorably, the persons we are. Adult sureness gives way to childhood fears. Routines break down. Weaknesses are exposed. Strengths are tested—and pass or fail with awful realness.

In the face of such loss—the loss of a piece of us, the loss of a child—there can be no safe havens. Our histories, our frailties, our deepest fears, become us.

15

Ted Prince is talking about the best years of his life. There have been many.

"I remember a time, when I was a young boy during the war —my grandfather, my aunt and uncle and us, we all lived on the same street. It was a lotta fun. Everywhere you looked, there were cousins.

"And on the same block, there was this retired admiral— 'The mayor of Chevy Chase,' we used to call him. He'd have all the war brides over for cocktails. . . .

"Our neighborhood postman, he used to read the postcards that would come from the men at the front—he must have been a talker, I guess, because everyone had all the news. . . .

"And the summers. My maternal grandfather—I was named

for him, he was head engineer for the New Haven Water Company, there's a building dedicated to him there—he lived on this farm outside New Haven. It had a tennis court, a croquet court, a seven-hole golf course, little ponds and oases everywhere. He designed it all himself. . . .

"And every June, as soon as the weather got warm enough to create a polio scare—well, we'd all just head north for the farm, stay there right through August. I spent all my summers there as a kid, from the late thirties till probably around 'forty-seven. . . .

"My grandfather and I, we *did* things together—tennis, golf, croquet. Whatever there was to do. Even toward the end, when he was sick [he died in 1952], I remember him going out and hitting baseballs to me. . . .

"I can't really remember any conversations I had with him —I just remember *doing* things. . . ."

Ted Prince sits at the desk of his law office on the ninth floor of the old Greyhound building in downtown Washington. He is a senior partner in the firm: Cushman, Darby and Cushman, specialists in patent and trademark law. He joined it at twenty-five, six months out of law school, and has been there since. He is fifty-six today.

It is a large room, formal but warm in its way, of dark wood and pale carpeting. The walls are hung sparingly with the small reminders of a well-rewarded life: a law degree from the University of Virginia, a bachelor's from Yale, a father-son tennis trophy, several color photos of the New Hampshire lake whose shore is the setting for the family's summer home.

At the corner of the desk, set apart from the sheaves of files and papers that cover much of the rest of the room, is a small

framed snapshot of Ted Prince's youngest son: in shoulder
pads and stained white jersey, between halves of a prep school
football game, two years before his death.

He tells me now about his father: about how, from the start
of his own law career in the early sixties until the older man's
retirement in 1975, the two lawyers, nearly every weekday
morning, would share a car to work, from their homes half a
mile apart in Chevy Chase to their offices in Washington's
downtown.

On the weekends, through those years, the two men played
doubles: tennis in the summer, paddle tennis once the weather
turned cold. At the Chevy Chase Club for several seasons, they
were unstoppable; once, in a father-son tournament that drew
entrants from nine states, they finished as runners-up.

Gregory Prince, now eighty-four, lives today with his second
wife in Ponte Vedra, Florida. He has Parkinson's disease and
is confined to a wheelchair, but his mind and will remain
strong. The two men talk weekly.

"Life is like that," Ted Prince says now, and smiles. "It's
made up of all sorts of little chapters. They open, they close,
and you go on."

Life, with one brutal exception, has been uncommonly kind to
this man. He has moved through it—been *borne* through it, it
would almost seem—buffered at every turn by all the blessings, natural and bestowed, that boy or man could ask. Wealth,
standing, tradition, a family's love, the best schooling money
could buy. There were no divorces or scandals, or mental
illness, or alcoholic black sheep. No one raised a hand in
anger; no one failed or cuckolded; there were no untimely
deaths.

For three generations at least, the anchors and landmarks stayed put. Children thrived and were praised for their thriving; parents and grandparents fostered, worked, grew old, and slowly died. Honor was a watchword. Love and kindness were practiced, planted, seldom or never discussed. It was a family like few today: a family that believed in itself, in the strengths and duties of blood.

Ted Prince's paternal grandfather, Sydney Rhodes Prince—"a formal sort of man, I never saw him without a suit and vest, smoking a cigar"—made a modest fortune, first in Alabama, later in Washington, as vice president and general counsel of Southern Railroad. On his farm in Greensboro, North Carolina, he kept a stableful of ponies for his grandchildren to ride; on Sunday afternoons at his Chevy Chase house, he hosted formal family lunches at which Ted, a young boy, refilled the glasses of his elders from seltzer bottles that squirted and fizzed— "I got such a kick out of that." He died when his grandson was ten.

His son, Ted's father, Gregory Smith Prince, was born in 1910, educated at the same Virginia boarding school to which his own two sons would later go, and then—again, in family fashion—at Yale. Like his father before him and his older son a generation hence, he would make his living as a lawyer, though not before serving through the war years as a supply officer in Portugal and South America.

He had married by then: to Margaret Eastman Minor, the daughter of the New Haven engineer at whose farm young Ted would later spend his summers. Their wedding took place there, in the fall of 1934. Ted, the firstborn, named for his mother's father, arrived three years later; the second and last child, Gregory, his father's namesake, came two years after that.

"My mother was the backbone. She did everything—ran the family, paid the bills, did the taxes, and still found time to hit tennis balls with us just about anytime we asked, during the war years when my dad was away."

The peace won, Gregory Prince returned home to Chevy Chase, to his two young boys and his wife. His older son was eight when his father came home. It was the start of a bond that would last half a century, shape much of the man the boy would become, and continue a legacy that would bestow on three more children, a generation hence, the gifts of love and family that only two of them would live to carry on.

Still too small to play golf with the grown-ups, young Ted tagged along behind his father on the course, until the day he was invited to play. After that, they were a twosome—when they weren't on the tennis court playing father-son doubles, or tossing baseballs, or away together on some family trip, of which there were many during the years when the boys were growing up.

"In our family, through the generations, that's the way it's always been. The values we have, the things we believe in—it just all comes out of being together, out of doing things together."

Dinner, every night, was a family affair: cooked and served by Mary Campbell, who prepared the meals for thirty years of Princes and would outlive some of those she served. But not Gregory Prince—who would bury his wife twenty years later and his youngest grandchild a generation after that.

The years passed. The family prospered. Ted, in fifth grade, was enrolled at private school. Four years later, he left home for Woodberry Forest, his father's alma mater, where he attended chapel four times weekly, played number one on the school's tennis team, and never ranked lower than third in his class. The Woodberry honor code, he remembers today, was a "defining influence" in his life.

"I was a happy kid. I played golf; I played tennis; I played basketball. I might have been okay at football too, but I lost a tooth playing in the seventh grade and I figured it was time to quit. . . ."

In the fall of 1955—in keeping with a tradition that had begun as long as two hundred years earlier, when an ancestor had founded its medical school—Ted Prince began his freshman year at Yale.

Four years later, he finished: with honors in civil engineering, a varsity tennis letter, and the school forever in his heart. All three of his children—he may have known this even then—would attend it. All three, like their father, would distinguish themselves—though the final distinction of the youngest Prince, as Yale's first murder victim in sixteen years, would close the fourth generation of family alumni with a grotesqueness that makes thoughts of a fifth seem, at least for the moment, obscene.

Ted and Sally Prince met in St. Anthony's Hall, on the University of Virginia campus in Charlottesville, on a Sunday afternoon in the spring of 1960. He was finishing his first year at law school; she was a junior at Sweet Briar, an hour south, and had arrived for dinner with a date.

"I took a long look at her. She was cute, and she was blonde—but she had a drink in one hand and a cigarette in the other, and that really wasn't my idea of the ideal girl."

He asked her out anyway, soon afterward—"my second

choice," he says today. "My first was busy that night." She
accepted, then accepted a second time. Six weeks later, as
planned, she left the States for a summer job at a hotel in
Bavaria. A month after her departure, Ted Prince, smitten by
now as he had never been before, called and proposed by
phone. She said no, then no again, then yes. They were married ten months later, in Staunton, Virginia, in June of 1961, a
week after her graduation from Sweet Briar. The bride was
twenty-one, the groom two years older.

So far as I know, I have never been witness to a marriage
made in heaven. But I have never, either—to the extent I am
privy to what goes into such things—seen a stronger one than
theirs. There is no magic to it. If it were a fabric, I might call it
sailcloth; as a house, it would be square with low ceilings and
walls of red brick.

They had been married sixteen months when Jackie was
born, in October 1962—with Khrushchev's ships, missile-
laden, steaming toward Cuba and the world on the edge of
war. Ted, who'd won his law degree four months before,
was an Army reservist at the time, on alert at Virginia's Fort
Eustus ("Bands playing, wives crying, it was scary stuff"),
and wouldn't see his firstborn until she'd been in the world
a week.

The crisis passed, the reservists came home. The new baby
was fat and healthy. New Year's came, and three days later
Ted's first and only job: at $6,500 a year, doing patent
searches at a shared desk in a crowded room.

They bought a home: big enough for three—then four—with

a tree out back that young Jackie—in her thirties today, soon
to have her own new husband and home—can still remember
falling from. They would stay there eight years, through two
children, until the week before Christian's arrival made them
five—then leave for the house on Longfellow Place, in which
they would still be living twenty years later, when they got the
news that made them four again.

Thirty years. Three children, two homes, one marriage, one
job. Continuity. Permanence. Commitment. A sense of tomorrow that gives today, in the best or worst of times, its dignity
and reasons for being.

Not long ago, Jackie Prince remembers, a longtime family
friend left his wife of many years for a younger woman. "My
father never talks about other people's business. But this time
was different—he was appalled. 'Disgusting,' 'awful,' 'unacceptable'—he used all those words. It was so odd, almost eerie, to hear him talk that way. . . .

"But for him, in the view he takes of things, you marry
one person for the rest of your life, for better or worse. It's a
simple way of looking at things—some people would call it
old-fashioned, and maybe it is. I've come to see it as in-
tegrity.

"I never felt, growing up, that we were any different from
any other family—except that my friends were always telling
me what a 'model relationship' my parents had. I'd come back
from vacation or something, and one of them would always be
asking, 'So, how are your parents these days?—God, they're
incredible.'

" 'Yeah,' I'd say, 'yeah, they're fine. My mom's busy at her
shop, and my dad's playing in some tournament or something.'
It all just seemed so natural to me. . . .

"But now, looking back, of my four closest friends in high

school—one set of parents is divorced, another is separated, the other two are unhappy, messed up. . . .

"It's amazing I took it all so for granted. . . ."

There were never many rules. There never seemed much need. Curfews were loose, unless abused; family dinners, as often as not, were reheated leftovers in the dining room or by the pool. Someone, nearly always, was coming or going from tennis or golf.

Teddy coached Christian, then rivaled him, until finally— just once—the younger boy won. Jackie came and went with boyfriends; Sally cooked and chauffeured, and dragged the children to museums, until—by the time the older two were driving—she began opening new stores. ("She was never much for baking cookies," her daughter says today.) Backpacks sat for days unemptied, Yale applications—three times in nine years—drew mealtime reassurances from Ted (just in case) about the legions of worthies who'd failed to make the grade.

"We had fun together," Jackie says. "We laughed a lot. We enjoyed each other, we teased each other, and got teased in return. Dad especially—he was always so traditional, the easiest target of all."

He is a traditional man. As his father was, and his father's father. He believes, as they did, in the sanctity of family, the power of constancy to preserve and provide, the passing down of honor without words.

Some would call him simple. By this they might mean that his tastes are not eclectic, or that his values derive from a prep school honor code, or that he lives an unexamined life.

But the world is full of examined lives that drown in their own examining; of failures, infidels, and alcoholics who moralize—miserably, pointlessly—without end. My own father was one of them, and scores of fathers, wives, and husbands I have known. Some would say, without cruelty, that I am one myself.

Such people are complex, "modern" men and women who search ceaselessly for meanings that often seem close at hand —but seldom bring peace and almost never add a shred of comfort to the lives of those who come after. "Meaning," after all, is rarely imparted on a grandfather's knobby knee.

For Ted Prince, life has never seemed a riddle. It is parceled out, he says, in "little chapters" from which he draws happiness, indifference, or despair—but makes no attempt to decipher or transcend. Luckier than most of us in the history he brings with him, he sees no reason to cast his nets beyond.

"My life, you might say, is kind of a rerun of my parents', and of their parents' before them. It's the only way I know—I was *born* to it. I suppose I'm someone who doesn't like a lot of change."

It's not that simple, as surely he knows. Human lives do not rewind and replay in the fashion of a VCR. But the values that shape them, if they are strong and uncorrupted, bring more comfort than pain and are practiced through action over time —these, at least, can be taught. Passed on by example, imbued in the fiber of a family, as pigment gives color to paint.

"I guess you'd call it a 'work ethic,' " Jackie Prince says today of her father's moral code. "He rarely set ultimatums; he almost never raised his voice" (only once at her that she can remember, when she'd somehow walked off with all four sets of keys to the family car), "but you always knew where he stood on things, and where you stood with him. . . .

" 'Do the fair thing,' 'Try your hardest,' 'You have to prac-

tice if you're going to be good.' He never made decisions for us
—personal responsibility was always the goal. But, for me at
least, he set the tone. . . ."

There is a doorjamb outside a bedroom of the Princes' New
Hampshire summer home. The heights of each child—and
both parents—are recorded there in pencil through the years.
"Once Christian got to be about sixteen," his father says—and
chuckles, fondly, at the thought—"I knew my time was running short. So I was planning to stretch out on the floor, to
my full height, to beat gravity, and have it measured that way.
It was a last resort, I knew. In the end it was a losing
cause. . . ."

On long family trips, there was the "Car Rule": the tallest
two in front, the others in the backseat, where the legroom was
never ideal. "And that left Teddy, once Christian passed him
by, in back by himself with the girls. It galled him, it really
did, to be kicked to the back by his little brother—but that's
the way it worked. . . ."

In the late summer of 1989 or 1990—Ted Prince can't remember which—Christian returned from two weeks at a tennis
camp, his skills at an all-time peak.

"He came back, and right then, the very first day, he went
out and played his brother—he'd never beaten Teddy before.
They played on hard courts—Christian's choice, he'd been
playing on hard courts every day at camp. . . .

"And I'm sitting up there, with Jackie and Sally, watching
the two of them going at it—it was a real close match. Christian won it, barely, in three sets. . . .

"Well, the next day, of course, they had to do it again—only
this time on clay courts. Teddy clobbered him.

"They were competitive, very competitive. But they loved to play *together*, too. . . .

"They used to challenge the boys across the street—play as a team, the two of them, for cases of beer. I thought that was wonderful. . . ."

On the morning of March 21, 1991, barely a month after his son had been slain, Ted Prince—his face ashen, speaking sometimes through tears—was on the floor of the United States Congress, testifying in support of the Brady Bill. His words, typewritten in advance, filled nearly seven pages. But he needed only twenty—the first twenty he spoke—to explain why he had come. "The Brady Handgun Violence Prevention Act is so simple, so morally right, that one wonders what the controversy is about."

Simple. Inarguable. Morally right. To the tallest goes the legroom. Handguns have no business on the street. In Ted Prince's world, you don't turn over rocks in search of truths— but when you find them, and they are plain to you, you don't call them by any other name.

"I've heard all the theoretical grounds, all the arguments [in favor of handguns]. All I can do is look 'em in the eye and say, 'You just don't understand what it's like; you just don't understand at all.' "

More than two years later, the Brady Bill still unpassed (it will be passed eleven months later), he sits rock-faced in a courtroom, eyes closed and knuckles, white as piano keys, gripping the back of the bench in front of him, listening to the "forensic details" of his son's last seconds on earth. He is in unimaginable pain. But he has come back—his second time in a year, alone this time, without his family for support—to bear witness to a spectacle that would tear the heart from any parent on earth.

Why? I ask. Why a second time? What cause does it serve to bear such torment? What possible difference could it make?

The question seems briefly to confuse him. He pauses, is for a moment lost for words. When he answers, I understand that it is not the question at all that has troubled him—it is my need, knowing him as I should by now, to ask it.

"I *had* to be there—for *him,* not me. I'm his father, his protector. That's what a father is."

16

It's three weeks before Christmas 1992, three months before Dunc Fleming's second trial. He's been in jail nineteen months, almost to the day—though by his count, he gets credit for twenty.

"You don't count a year January to January—May to April, now *that's* a year. I been in twenty months. Any way you figure it, it's a year and some change gone outta my life. I gotta make up for that."

He sits across from me at a visitor's table, one of two that run nearly the length of the room—which is cavernous and dreary, but spotlessly clean. At my back, two inmates, moving as if half-alive, spray small squirts of Windex onto a display case, wipe weakly, and move on. On the far wall, a massive red-and-blue mural—an eagle and flag—honors the triumph (and presumably the victims) of Desert Storm. Next to it, a poster-sized notice—large block lettering, once each in English and Spanish—announces the rules: Nothing, it says, is to pass between inmate and visitor, and no objects—"including infants"—are at any time to be placed on the tables they share.

Up and down the rows, pale, ruttish teenage couples grope and paw across and under tables; two chairs down from us, a two-year-old clings to her mother's leg and wails.

What will you do when you get out? I want to know. How will you make up for the time?

"Just hang out. Ride around with the boys, pick up some girls at the mall maybe, maybe get high once in a while."

And after that? A job, a future, a family—the things you think of when you're lying in bed at night?

"I'd maybe like to take a cruise—I never done that before. The Bahamas maybe, the Caribbean. Just lie out on some island, spend a whole day just sittin' out on some beach somewhere, nothin' to do, nowhere to go—maybe get a tan if I wanted."

He laughs as he says this, a small, almost soundless little laugh. In the distance, as though in answer, a police siren wails briefly, then dies.

"You always hearin' that in here," he tells me. "After a while, you get so you don't hear it no more."

He has just turned eighteen. He has changed since they took his picture for the *Times* six or seven months before. He is no longer bald, though his hair remains short and tight to his head. He seems thinner now, but no less muscled: A hundred or more afternoons in the prison's weight room have chiseled and hardened him. And the inmate "intramurals"—basketball and football, one "cottage" against the next—have kept him fit, he says.

He still has his mustache, and the beginnings of what could only be called a goatee. His hands and fingers are long and graceful, almost elegant. They could be a pianist's. His eyes are soft, sometimes dreamy, and almost never meet mine. He shifts constantly in his chair—less from discomfort, it seems, than impatience—and offers a wave to any inmate who glances his way.

"I got *friends* in here," he tells me. "I know probably every guy in this room."

Christian Prince's killing is off-limits as a subject: the bargain struck with Dunc's attorney as a condition for my visitor's pass. For me, it's a small sacrifice. His denial is a matter of record and will be upheld or disproven, in any case, in three months' time.

But Dunc, plainly, is at a loss. What else could there be to talk about? Why else would I be here? He says nothing of this —only sits mute between questions and searches the room with his eyes, as though the answer to my presence might hang somewhere in the air.

I ask about his days, his duties and routines. He goes to school weekday mornings, he says. "Just like regular school, math and language arts and stuff." And on Wednesdays, computer lab.

He's working toward his GED. "With the lost time and all, it oughtta take about two years."

In the afternoons, he works—"mostly moppin' and cleanin'

and washin' windows and all, but they give me twenty bucks or somethin' every coupla weeks."

He's applying for a new job, he tells me: "Somethin' outside of F Cottage, somethin' with more movement, less moppin', more people around."

He is such a boy.

We talk of his family. His father's mother down south: "She keep you laughin', make you happy just talkin' to her." They talk by phone, he says, every four or five weeks.

His father: "Me and my pops—he more like a friend, you know, like the same age or somethin'. We just talk like regular —he tell me, like, some girl I know just stopped by, or maybe some home boy he ain't seen for a while, he want to know if maybe he show up here. Just regular talk, you know, just two guys talkin'."

He tells me something I hadn't known but probably should have: that the first and third floors of the Fleming walk-up on Winchester Avenue—Jim and Julia live on the second—are rented by cousins and aunts. "A family home," he calls it, and seems proud, the prouder when he learns I hadn't know before.

"A family *sandwich*," I answer. And he laughs and repeats this: " 'A family sandwich'—I like that, man, that's pretty good."

Girls are a favorite subject—though not the way you'd probably think.

"You can't trust 'em. They know you in jail, don't know how much time you doin'—'Oh, I love you, I love you,' they be sayin'.

"The next day, just like that, they be with somebody else. You can't trust 'em, man. I don't even call 'em no more."

The last time he was "serious," he tells me, was when he was fifteen.

"It was with this girl from 'round my way. We was doin' it, y'know, havin' sex. Then I got shot—couldn't walk or nothin' for like six, seven months, didn't hardly see her at all. . . .

"Then, like bang—she have this baby. 'You *it,*' she tell me. 'You the father,' she say.

" 'If I be the father,' I tell her, 'then why you stop comin' 'round?' She never could tell me that.

"For a long time, I used to stand in front of the mirror just holdin' that baby—'Is you my baby? Is you my baby?' I be sayin'. . . .

"And everybody else, y'know, everybody tellin' me, 'That baby got your nose, got your eyes and all'—and pretty soon I be believin' it myself.

"Then one day, just like that, she take up with some kid from KSI—and suddenly it's *his* baby, ain't my baby no more."

I ask about sex in general. As a subject, I can plainly see— from the first moment he opens his mouth—it is far less awkward for him than for me.

"DAMN! First time I had it, I guess, was fourth grade—I was hangin' around with this older guy, you know. He was seventeen or something, a whole lot older than me. . . .

"Anyway, he took me ridin' 'round and all—schooled me on all that stuff, on all that sex and shit. At first, you know, I was pretty bugged out. But it got easy. Before long, I be pushin' up on girls. . . ."

But don't you ever worry? I ask him. About who you "push up on," about where she's been, about where she's going from you? Do you ever use condoms? Do you ever think about that stuff? I am as bumbling and nervous, in asking all this, as if I were eighteen myself.

"Shit. You talkin' about *AIDS?* Half of New Haven probably have AIDS. All the girls be fuckin', everybody fuckin'. I got it, I sure as hell don't want to know."

His time here in Cheshire, he tells me, "ain't really so bad . . . kinda wild sometimes, though—it's easy to get in trouble, you gotta watch your step."

Not long ago, he says, he lost his privileges—table hockey, gym trips, phone time, an hour of evening rec—because he stood up without permission in the dining hall at breakfast one day. "I was laughin', man, at some dude's joke, laughin' so hard I thought I was gonna be sick. So I got up to keep from throwin' up my food. And for that, man—for *that*—they took away my time."

He is gaining focus now. He is angry. His voice rises and hardens. The dreaminess goes out of his eyes. The boy is gone, displaced by something else. Not a man, certainly—but nothing you could call a child.

"The system, man—the system is so *fucked.* Inside, outside, it's the same either way. I seen a lotta foul stuff, you wouldn't believe. . . .

"You wanna talk about *racism?* There was this white guy— this white guy in court one day, you know? Well, it's like his fourth arson—four times this dude's been pulled in for burnin' things down.

"So what do they give him? A PTA [Promise to Appear]—a PTA, four fuckin' arsons and the guy gets off with a PTA. . . .

"And *me?* I get a million-dollar bond. A million-dollar bond —for murder, man, for murder. I never in my life seen anything like it."

. . .

What about drugs? I ask him.

He loses interest. His voice goes flat again; his eyes resume their listless search. "Don't sell 'em—never have, never will. I got too much respect for my pops be doin' that shit—can't be sellin' that stuff right out there on the corner, right under his nose. It's about respect, man."

But most of your friends are selling it, aren't they? And aren't a lot of them dead?

He lowers his head and begins counting on his fingers: "Tazio, Grimlock . . . only about eight, I think, maybe nine, maybe not that many. . . .

"It's a *business,* man, a business. How come none of you guys can get that right?

"Let's say you gotta little hardware store. That's your job, right? That's how you get by—and somebody else, he be sellin' used tools right out in front of your store. . . . Well, you gonna want to *get* him, right? And probably he gonna want to get you, too. Somebody gonna get killed either way. . . ."

Our conversation shifts. Your fondest memories? I ask him. The happiest moments, the times you treasure most?

This stops him. He is silent, almost motionless, for half a minute or more. And then, for what may be the first and only time, he looks straight at me, meeting my eyes with his own. His voice drops and softens to something like a purr: "Tichelle," he says simply. And pauses again.

"My first niece, y'know—Tanya's little girl. She's four years old; her name's Tichelle.

"I got to hold her, just hold her"—he makes a cradling motion with his arms, so awkwardly gentle, so incongruous, that for a moment I'm not certain just what it is I'm seeing—

"and play with her, and throw her in the air and catch her and make her squeal and laugh. . . .

"When she was just a baby, right after she was born? The days when I had to be in school? Well, I'd be sittin' there all day long, just lookin' at the clock, waitin' for the time to be done, so I could go home and play with my little Tichelle.

"I be missing her, just missing her so bad, just about all the time. . . .

"And sometimes now, y'know, on nights when I get to call home? Sometimes she be the one that answers the phone. And she say 'yes' to the charges, all by herself—'yes, ma'am,' she say, to the operator on the line. And her bein' only four years old and all. . . .

"It make me feel real proud—like being a daddy or somethin', I guess."

The archetypal street punk, as most any big-city social worker will tell you these days, is a loveless, fatherless, sometimes motherless, high school dropout whose family—such as it is—live in chronic, indifferent poverty; whose principle caretaker (if there is one) is as likely as not to be an addict; who's beaten regularly at home—and often abused sexually—has had little or no exposure to the values of family, community, church, or school; and whose central message from the world is that it has less than no use for him.

"The truth behind some of these lives is horrific, beyond what most people could grasp," says Ellen Knight, a social anthropologist in the Hartford Public Defender's office whose caseload is so ridden with horror stories it's hard to imagine how she manages to get out of bed every day.

"The worst of it is, you never even learn the *whole* truth.

Most of these people, they'd rather die than let you know—
'Yeah, everything's just fine,' they say. 'No problems, everything's just fine. . . .'

"Well, you want to know what 'fine' really means? 'Fine' is
when everybody's sleeping with everybody else's brothers and
sisters and fathers—and this person doesn't really know who
his father is, the daughter's sleeping with the mother's boyfriend, the kids are stabbing their parents. . . .

"There's no heat; there's a stench in the place you wouldn't
believe; the roaches are crawling all over your feet; there's
two-day-old food in the sink, rotten eggs in the fridge—and the
mother, meanwhile, is smacking the kid around.

"But everything's always 'fine, just fine. . . .' "

Dunc Fleming's life doesn't fit this mold. His parents are
together, and have been for as long as he's known. Neither
one, from all I can tell, has ever had a problem with drugs.
And although poor today, and sick and unemployed, Jim
Fleming—for eleven of Dunc's eighteen years—earned a
decent, dependable wage in a job that made him a hero
to his son.

There are no signs of violence. The family apartment is
cramped and less than tidy, but there are no rats or roaches in
sight. Both parents, at least half of the time, used to go to
church on Sundays, as did Dunc himself—who also managed,
until jail interrupted it, to get through nearly ten years of
school.

When you ask him to describe his values, he dutifully re-
cites those of his "pops": "Don't steal. Stay in school. Respect
my elders. Don't do no drugs. Stay away from the wrong
crowd."

■ ■ ■

This is a boy who worships his father, goes wet eyed over
boasts of his niece, talks unashamedly about God, has spent
all but his last Christmas unwrapping presents under the family tree—and would probably rather, if you asked him to
choose, eat macaroni and chicken in his mother's kitchen than
anyplace else on earth.

But he's in jail: convicted of one crime and (although he'll
be acquitted of them) charged with two more. And he's been
there before: for car theft in early 1991, breach of peace a year
earlier. He was shot through both legs at fifteen—"that's when
the bad luck started," he says—shaken down by police for
drugs and guns, transferred between schools as a protection
against gangs. Most of his friends are drug dealers—"busi-
nessmen," as he would say—and nearly all have done time. At
least eight he can think of are dead. He figures it's about fifty-
fifty he won't last ten more years himself.

"He's a walking bomb," says Frank Iannotti, the man who
defended him in court. "An angry kid—it's only a matter of
time."

Why? Anger at what? What would cause a sixteen-year-old
boy, raised on old-fashioned values, with a loving family to go
home to at night, to set out instead at one in the morning with a
gun in his pocket to "rob a cracker" on the campus of a
school?

On a weekend afternoon, sometime in the mideighties, around
the time, as his father recalls today, that his tastes in TV began
their shift from the Road Runner to Bruce Lee—"and Arnold
Schwarzenegger, and all that kinda stuff"—Dunc was playing
with some friends at the neighborhood's Ivy Park.

He remembers, he says, being "eight or nine" at the time—

though that would have been a year or more before the start of the city's cocaine boom. It's more likely he was ten.

An older boy—"fifteen, sixteen, maybe more"—was shooting hoops at the other end. "It was a drive-by. Coupla shots, like firecrackers goin' off—and the kid, he just drops to the ground, they got him in the jaw. That was the first guy I saw die."

More shootings followed. The cocaine trade, by the late eighties, had carved the city into turfs. Death became commonplace, then heroic. All across Newhallville, the street names of the dead boys began appearing as graffiti on storefronts and sidewalks, sometimes with hearts around them, as though written between lovers. On Dunc's block of Winchester Avenue, in the space of two years, six young black boys lost their lives to guns.

Little Tichelle, two years old at the time, would wake up nights when the shooting started and run to her grandparents' bed. " 'Pow-pow, Nana, pow-pow, I scared,' " Jim Fleming remembers—"that's exactly what she'd say."

For Dunc—as for thousands of others like him throughout the city, as for soldiers in wartime or victims of a siege—life, in the space of not much more than a year, reduced itself to a contest between fear and will. He knew, or sensed, probably by the time he'd turned twelve, that he would have to make a choice.

I don't know Dunc Fleming, but I know one thing," says Tim Shriver, a former teacher and now superintendent of social development for New Haven schools. "He feels, he fears, he thinks, he loves, he hates, and all the rest, just like you and I. . . ."

The lives of ghetto children, Shriver says, evolve in grim,

predictable stages—from innocence, through terror, to survival.

"The younger ones, the little ones—they're all pretty much the same. They all watch *Sesame Street* and love Big Bird; they all wait for Santa Claus every year—just innocent, sweet, trusting little kids. . . .

"Then, as they get into their early teens, they become *overwhelmed* by fear. . . . It's a high-stakes game in the ghetto; there's no safe place to go, no place to rest your head emotionally. . . .

"The white world is unavailable; your peer group is scary; the world of Mom and Dad is unfamiliar, often grim. There's no middle ground. You either join a gang or you side with Grandma. Either way, you put up barriers, you survive, you get through."

And whatever the choice—Shriver is very quick to add—whatever the consequences, however many Christian Princes get murdered or Dunc Flemings go to jail: "Guilt—their guilt, our guilt, anybody's guilt—has nothing to do with the point. These are *kids* we're talking about here—not hateful, barbaric, maiming lunatics. These are *kids*, for Christ's sake, these are kids."

When Dunc was thirteen, his curfew was moved back: from six o'clock to eight, then nine. He got down with the Lynch Mob—a young-teen posse, apprentices to the 'Ville—then with the 'Ville itself. He got shot; he got busted; he "pushed up" on girls; he learned (if he hadn't learned already) to handle a twenty-two.

Whether he sold drugs or used them, and he swears he did neither (" 'cept for reefer now and then"), he had found his answer to the fear. His life, irrevocably by the time he'd turned fourteen, was on the street.

"It's my place, man. It's family; it's all I know. The boys there—they the brothers I don't got. Big brothers, little brothers, from Winchester all the way down to Shelton—family people, family-type relationships, you know what I'm sayin'?

"We hang together, we *do* stuff together—maybe go for a ride, go to the mall, catch a movie now and then. We take *care* of each other, man, watch out for each other, like brothers are s'posed to do. . . ."

He offers an example. Three years ago, he says, when his girlfriend got pregnant, the brothers were there for him. Or would have been, if he'd needed them to be.

"That baby turn out to be mine? No way I just walk away from that, man, no way. I be the father, I bear the load—get together fifteen hundred at least, maybe more, have it delivered right at her door, take care of that kid.

"That money's there, man. All I got do is ask. I told you— we *family*, we look out for each other. . . .

"Or like, say, if I was to get jumped in the mall? What I gonna do? I put a call in—I say, 'Yo, guys, I just got beat down in the mall; load up the posse and come take care of it.'

"And they *come*, man—I call, they come. Just like I would for a brother, just like I would for them. Like I say, it's family time. . . ."

17

His street name is Merlin. I don't know his real one. He is a "brother," one of Dunc's closest, a 'Ville Boy since sixteen, the same year he dropped out of school.

He is twenty today; tall and handsome with smooth skin and broad shoulders, a gimpy leg from a fall he took a week ago in a race with a cop, and a smile I keep mistaking for a sneer. He is smart, quick-witted, and utterly without reserve, as cocky as a linebacker in a bar of fifty-cent toughs.

His eyes are steely and very, very dark, and seem to exist as much to challenge as to see. His wit is sharp and often funny, but as black as the shirt on his back. He *hates* the world and wants you to know it—but only, he would tell you, because it hated him first.

Merlin deals drugs for a living. He's been busted twice for possession with intent and has served a year of time. On the afternoon we get together, in late November of 1992, three months before Dunc's second trial, he's been out three months on parole.

I have asked to meet a dealer and have promised in return to write nothing that could disclose who he is. ("Merlin" is my creation, though I've tried to be true to the spirit of his name.) It has taken Tanya Fleming—who at nineteen seems able to walk out her door on Winchester Avenue and return with just about anything or anyone she wants—roughly ten minutes to produce one.

We are sitting—Merlin, Tanya, Jim Fleming, and I—in the family living room, discussing terms. It is understood between us, for starters, that Merlin doesn't deal drugs. It is also understood, of course, that he does.

S ay I was to be sellin'—just say I was. What does that make me? You say, 'Oh, man, it make him a *ga-aang member*, it make him a *dr-uhhhg addict.'*

"Ain't like that, man. People out there just tryin' to make a livin', they just tryin' to eat.

"It's crucial, man. You got guys out there that gotta pay rent, guys that got baby mothers, cryin' without diapers. Can't say no to that baby, that baby *want*, I'm sayin'?"

Merlin is good. A salesman—I can see that. And I'm the customer now.

There are other ways to make a living, I say.

"Shit. What you tellin' me? *Burger King?* Five-and-a-quarter an hour? That ain't money, man. . . .

"Let's say you gotta paper route, I'm sayin'? You got this

little paper route, and this other guy, he be sellin' drugs. And the day comes you get paid, and you be lookin' at your little bit o' money—Burger King kinda money, I'm sayin'?—and about that time that other guy come walkin' up, all dressed up, some good-lookin' girl wrapped 'round him, lookin' smart and all. . . .

"Well, what you gonna do? You start hangin' with him, right? You start bein' 'round him and all, and it's gonna come automatic—one day you be goin', 'Man, I'm gonna quit this here paper route, make me some *re-eel* money for a change.'

"That's how it is, man. You go where the money is—and the money is on the *street,* man, ain't nowhere but the street.

"You can try and stop it. You can arrest every nigger out there, arrest a hundred niggers today, tomorrow there be *two* hundred. . . . Everybody jus' waitin' for their chance."

If he were to sell coke, Merlin tells me, he'd sell it in ten-dollar bags, fifty bags to a bundle. On an average day, he might sell three bundles, on a good day ("the third and the sixteenth, when them welfare checks hit, that's when you make the *craa-zy* money") as many as six. His own take, he says, would range between $300 and $500 a day.

With that kind of money, he says, he'd be on top of the world.

"Buck-eighty for a pair of Timberlands, 'nother three, four hundred on the outfit I be gettin' for this fashion show next week—next Friday night, cross-color fashion show at the Park Plaza, pants, shirt, boots, the whole thing—'nother buck, buck-fifty make the girl look good. . . .

"I got it stashed all over, I'm sayin'? My sister's house, my mother's house—closets fulla stuff, got so many boots you wouldn't believe. . . ."

I ask Merlin how much cash he could lay his hands on right now. He looks at me through those steely black eyes, smiles his thin little sneer of a smile, and answers:

"Enough."

Enough for what? I want to know. Enough for a house, a car, enough to put away?

"Shit. You talkin' 'bout savin'? You don't know nothin', man, you don't know from *shit*. What's the use of me havin' ten, twenty thousand stashed and die tomorrow? You tell me, man —what's the use of that?"

Merlin lives with his mother when he isn't in jail. She is a line worker at a data processing firm in North Haven and "won't take a nickel" of the money he makes on the street. "A decent woman," he says.

"But she wasn't, you know, like ready for kids. But she didn't believe in abortion, so my grandmother had to take me for a while. So that answers your question 'bout how come I'm here."

He had a father once; "They was married for a while." He can't remember the last time he saw him. Months? I ask. Years? He shrugs.

This happens a lot. When a subject interests him, he has an answer for everything. When it doesn't, he mostly just shrugs.

Until he was ten, he tells me, he lived in South Carolina, with the grandmother who'd taken him in. "Then my mother came and got me. I wished I'd stayed down there."

In New Haven, he went to three schools in six years. By the time he dropped out, he says, roughly half his friends were making a living on the street. Of the other half, maybe a dozen were in jail. "Two or three," he says, were dead. It was still pretty early.

But all that aside, there was no good reason to stay in school. "The teachers, they don't teach you nothin'. Shit, man, they too *scared* to teach. They just tryin' to make it through the day."

Except for dealing, he's never worked a day in his life. "They punch in my Social Security number, it come up negative, man. Negative. No callouses. But I gotta job, too—on my feet all day sometimes, sometimes half the night. . . ."

That's about it for biography. Merlin's life story, by Merlin's telling, is a three-minute affair. So nugatory as a subject it scarcely rates the effort to recount. And when he does—or tries—it's plain that there's a link missing. As he speaks of the ten-year-old who came north from his grandmother's, his tone is so flat he could be reciting from a book.

"I don't think much 'bout that kinda stuff," he says.

He hasn't much to say, either, about his friend Dunc. Except that he's innocent: "Got jammed with one of those humbug things."

I ask how he can be so certain. At first he just stares at me. Then he shakes his head slowly and looks off into space. By the time he answers, I've stopped believing he will.

"Shit. Everybody knows—Yalies don't got no money. Ain't nobody don't know that. You rob a Yalie, what you gonna get? Maybe a hype CB jacket, a hype Black Ice, coupla dollars and change. Shit."

Merlin is angry, the angrier the longer we talk. And it doesn't have much to do with Dunc or Christian Prince or Yale—

except in the most literal sense—or anything else he thinks I want to talk about. It has to do with why I'm here in the first place.

"You the writer, right? You gonna write a book. And here you are, wantin' to talk to me about this murder, this *big-time*, prime-time murder. . . .

"A white kid got wasted, okay? A Yale kid. He dead, he ain't comin' back. And here are you, with your pencil and your notebook and your little black machine, wantin' to know all about what it's like—about what it's like to be *'on the street,'* *'dealin' drugs,'* all that good shit. . . .

"Fuck that, man. That ain't what you wanna know. You wanna know how come this white Yale kid is dead, and why some black guy killed him. That's all you wanna know. The *racial shit.* That's what you gonna write—just tell me I'm wrong, man. Tell me I'm wrong, I might believe you. . . ."

The racial shit. It's most of what he wants to talk about. He is poisoned by it. He sees it everywhere.

" 'White man murdered, news at six. . . .'

"Six o'clock come—'White man murdered, no suspects.' Leave it at that. . . .

" *'Black* man murdered—drug-related, gang-connected, possible gang warfare, bullshit-bullshit-bullshit.'

"They get all that outta one person gettin' killed—they make the black guy look so bad. The white guy, he coulda been a rapist, a murderer, a pervert who did little kids—they don't say *none* of that. Just go, 'Film at six, white man murdered, no suspects, film at six.'

"It's all *backwards,* man, it's all fuckin' backwards."

He is so angry now he is almost out of his chair: voice raised, arms waving, eyes flashing like strobes. I have the

thought that if he were white his face would be red by now—
and then that I have no idea if black faces turn red.

"You ever been in jail, man?"

I tell him no.

"I figured that. Well, let me tell you somethin' 'bout how
things go in jail. . . .

"Two black guys jump a white guy, right? You got outside
charges—assault first, 'tempt murder, all that kinda stuff. Two
white boys jump a black one—what you get then? Five days in
the hole, loss of a hundred twenty days good time, no TV for a
month. That's *all*, man, that's all.

"I seen it happen, man. I seen worse than that. The COs,
they shine lights in your face when you sleepin', they beat you
up if you bitch. . . .

"They *cut* you or somethin'? They leave you in the hole till
your scars heal. You could *die* in there, they don't give a shit.

"A black guy get stabbed in jail? They drag you to the
infirmary—they *drag* you, man. You dead, you dead. You alive,
you alive. Don't make no difference to them. . . ."

I have never, to my knowledge, been in the presence of
anyone with such a hatred of life. Listening to him, I feel
sometimes that I should plug my ears and look away. That I am
intruding on an indecency. That he would be better off dead.

But Merlin is twenty, an old man by the standards of the
street. He is Dunc in two years, if Dunc can make it that long.
He has earned his hatred. He's been jailed and rejailed, and
beaten up and shot at. He has a T-shirt covered, front and
back, with the names of dead friends: "Terry-O, Tyrone, Tazio,
Jerome, Jerome Young, Daniello, Grimlock, Mike Younger,
Kiddie Hazard . . .

"All dead, man, all shot, all of 'em shot. Crazy people, man,
crazy home boys . . ."

■ ■ ■

Our talk turns to death. Merlin tells me about his buddy Tyrone, shot dead a week ago at the Planet X.

"I told him, 'Don't go, man, don't go near that place. It's gonna be *crucial*, man. That place is tight, man. They got no security there.'

"White people have a party, I'm sayin'? There be *crazy* security, cops all over the place. Party in a black neighborhood? Police go, 'fuck it, let 'em kill themselves. . . .'"

And the maimed but still living. A boy named Girard: "Shot like seven, eight times—he *still* got a bullet in his back and a bullet in his neck."

And another boy he doesn't name, shot and paralyzed, a cripple in a wheelchair: "But that don't stop 'em—they shot him two more times after he was in the chair, still don't kill him. They'll prob'ly try again pretty soon."

Jim Fleming has been listening quietly through all of this, nodding, then shaking his head, then nodding some more. He looks now as if he might be about to cry.

"I tell you what I think. My boy James? He be in the best place he could be. If he was to be here right now? If he was to be on that street? One day, for sure, I'd be hearin' it—*BAM! BAM!*—and there'd be a flash of a gun, and then my son, lyin' there, stretched out dead on the street. . . ."

Merlin seems softened by this. For the first time in almost an hour, his anger lifts. He looks over at Dunc's father—who is seated in a chair between us, the stump of his missing left leg propped on a pillow in front of him—with a kindness that seems suddenly to have melted his rage.

"Naw, would'na gone that way with Dunc. He wasn't the

same way as them. He stayed in school, never got into no crazy stuff—he had respect for his pops, I'm sayin'?"

Jim Fleming smiles. "I'd surely like to believe that," he says.

Tanya reminds us all that there's still a trial coming up. "You all talkin' like he's dead and gone. He's been in jail two years. Two years—for nothin.' Nothin'. But the truth, it's bound to come out. . . ."

Merlin, for the moment, is subdued. Philosophical. The thoughts of his street-brother behind bars have put him in a different mind.

"I know one thing for sure. Down the line, I'm sayin'? Down the line, I don't get out of this, man? There's only two ways it can go. It's either jail or—the other one. I gotta get out. I gotta make a break some way.

"But you don't just come off, man. It ain't that easy. You gotta have a certain amount of money in your mind, a certain game plan.

"I *used* to have a game plan. Problem is, you can't *stick* with no game plan. . . .

"You get that money, I'm sayin'? You go, 'Whoa, I just made all this, right here in this little bit of time—I *know* I can make more. . . . You get greedy. You *chase* that money. And anybody knows, you chase money, only bad things come.

"But *shit*, man, think about it, just *think* about it. You pay six-fifty an ounce in the city; here you sell it for eight-fifty, maybe nine hundred—that's close to three hundred profit. And if you cut it [with lactose], weigh it, grind it, sift it, and bag it all up, you can get eighteen, nineteen hundred an ounce. . . .

"There's thirty-six ounces in a key, man. Add it up, man.

Add it up. And all you gotta do is sit there. Just sit there and wait. . . .

"What you gonna do? You be a *damn fool* to say no. . . ."

It is this thinking, more or less, that is ravaging black teenage (and family) life in cities from New York to Los Angeles. "You be a *damn fool* to say no"—you could drive down any street of any ghetto in America at noon on a schoolday and pass boy after boy who lives by this creed. There are no numbers kept on how many have died in its name. Certainly thousands. Tens of thousands more have been wounded, many permanently. Hundreds of thousands, probably millions, have dropped out of school to stand on street corners with glassine bags: to "just sit there and wait" for the cars with the twenty- and fifty-dollar bills to make them rich enough to buy sneakers and jackets with price tags so obscene they mock the reality of a mother's welfare check.

In Newhallville, in the Dixwell section, near Quinnipiac Terrace, and at a half-dozen other sites around town, there is an open market on every other corner—and hundreds of boys who wouldn't be anywhere else on a Friday or Saturday night. The millions of dollars they make in a year—and it is *many* millions—like most dollars earned anywhere, find their way back to the city's merchants and malls.

Car dealers, clothing stores, novelty shops (especially the kind that offer such items as crack pipes and triple-balance-beam scales), video stores, shoe stores, sporting goods outlets —a lot of them wouldn't survive without drug money. For some, it's as much as half the year's receipts.

In September 1990, a two-part *New Yorker* series included the story of Body and Sole, a sporting goods store on New Haven's Chapel Street that hoped to set an example by boycotting dealers:

"You can send a message to other kids—that not all the merchants in town are bending over to service the dealers, that the hypocrisy stops here," owner Wally Grigo told the *New Yorker*'s William Finnegan at the time. "Drug dealers are *not* legitimate business people. They're killing their own communities, and I'm not going to profit from them."

Not much more than a year later, Body and Sole was out of business. A competitor meanwhile, apparently less picky about the sources of its sales (it is Merlin's top choice when its comes time for a new pair of sneakers or boots), had expanded from one store to three.

"Man, how dumb is *that?*" says Merlin. "What you s'pose they think? That they was gonna make it offa *white people?* There *ain't* no white people out there spendin' no buck-fifty, buck-eighty on no pair of sneakers.

"The white man, he go out and buy a pair of Pro Keds for forty bucks—pair of Skippies, pair of Rockports or Converse. He buy straight. . . .

"You know who be buyin' the stuff costs the buck-fifty, buck-seventy-five? The *drug dealers,* man, that's who.

"So you gonna say no to drug money? Would *you?* Hell no, man, I sure wouldn't. That was the dumbest thing I ever seen.

"And while Body and Sole is sayin' that, Sports Stuff is goin', 'Come on, come on, we'll take your money.'

"*All* money is drug money in this town, man. One way or the other, legal or illegal. It either come off the street or it come from money that come from money that come off the street.

"It's all the same in the end, I'm sayin'? It all spins out the same way. It's all green, and it's all got dead presidents on the front. . . ."

He can make $300 any night he chooses, owns too many clothes and boots to house in a walk-in closet, and can have any girl he sets his sights on: "You just *look* like you got money, I'm sayin'? You got your pick of 'em. . . ."

But he's wretched. Scared and angry and lonely and full of hate. He misses the friends he's lost, can't trust the ones still left ("Can't trust *nobody*, man, everybody schemin' "), believes in nothing more than the wad of dollars in his pocket and resents his faith in those, and wouldn't give a nickel for his chances of making it to his thirtieth birthday free and alive and in one piece.

And it's no worse for him, he says, than for anyone else on the street. "Ain't *nobody* happy, man. Nobody. Don't never hear the word. You happy 'cause you ain't broke, I'm sayin'? But you ain't *happy-happy*, and you ain't never gonna be. . . ."

He'd trade it all, he swears—and I believe him, if it could be given on a plate—for "eight, maybe nine an hour, some benefits, a union, just knowin' I be sure to wake up the next day. . . . I be thinkin' that way sometimes, I'm sayin'? A job, a house, a car, maybe some little kids. Live life real pretty, real sweet."

Then he tells me about this dream he has. As dreams go, it doesn't seem improbable. Still, we've been together close to two hours by now, and he hasn't mentioned it once.

"Soon's this parole is up, I'm sayin'? This February comin'
up? Maybe I just be gettin' down south."

He tells me about a grandfather with a tobacco business in
South Carolina, a soft spot for his grandson, and a home big
enough to share. "Sure as shit," he says, "I ask for a job, he
give me one. I be *straight* then, man, I be outta here, I be livin'
my life."

I say this sounds perfect. Ideal. What's to stop you? And I
mean it. I find myself feeling—despite myself, despite my
"pencil and notebook and little black machine"—this rush of
quickened hope. Go for it, I want to tell him. Go for it right
now. I want to ask for his grandfather's number. I want to dial
it myself.

But it doesn't last. His very next breath negates it—and I
wish then instead, for a second at least, that I had never met
this boy.

"But they be sellin' down *there* too, man. Somebody tell me,
they be gettin' thirty, forty dollars a bag. Forty dollars—that's
money, man, that's money. It be *crucial* time down there."

Our time together is over. Merlin is on his feet. We shake
hands. I say good luck. He wants to know—"So when this
book of yours be out?"

Two years, I tell him. Maybe more.

"Two years?" he says. *"Two years?* Shit, man, the world
could end before two years."

Your world, maybe, I say—despite myself. My world will
still be here.

He laughs. His mouth, for the first time since our first minutes together, is back in its little sneer of a smile.

"Maybe you right, maybe you wrong. I guess you oughtta

know though, huh? You this big-time writer with all the answers—this big-time writer come down from New York or Boston or wherever you from, come to talk to Dunc and me and
Tanya and all the other niggers about this white boy gettin'
killed. . . .

" 'Tell me your thoughts,' you be sayin' all this time. 'Tell
me this, tell me that, tell me what you think.'

"That's bullshit, man, and you know it. You don't care
nothin' for what I think.

"Well, I got a question for *you,* man. I got the sixty-four-
thousand-dollar question. . . .

"Let's just say I was to be out there on that street—and I'm
sittin' there with no money and nothin' to eat, and you walk by
and I say to you, 'Yo, man, help me out, man, I need a dollar to
eat. . . .'

"What you think you gonna do?

"I *know* what you do—you could have a pocketful of money,
it don't make no difference. . . .

"You go, 'I don't got none.' Or else you gonna look at me,
then look away and pretend like you don't see nothin', you
don't see that poor nigger sittin' there, like I was invisible or
somethin'. And then you just keep on walkin'. . . .

"You lookin' at me like I'm *crazy,* man—but you *know* what
I'm sayin', you know it's the truth. Nobody give nobody nothin',
man. Nothin'. Tell me it ain't the truth. . . ."

I try not to tell him anything. But it's hard.

18

Not all of the letters the Prince family have saved bear condolences. Not all were even written, originally, for their eyes.

From a New York City woman, following the reporting of Dunc Fleming's first trial, to the editor of the *New York Times:*

> In your outrageous attempt to portray the vicious murder of Christian Prince as an inevitable outcome of class and racial disparity ("Son of Privilege, Son of Pain," 6/28/92), you gloss over several telling details. The reason that the Oasis, other juke joints and New Haven danger zones are "knotted with young men with no work to do" is that these underage teenage drinkers choose not to stay in school but to mug a "cracker" for some quick cash instead.

There is no work that society can concoct for unskilled, uneducated teenagers who join street gangs
and choose nicknames like Scarface and Thumbhead.
There is no deus ex machina for families in which 19-
year-old unmarried women already have two children,
and 16-year-old boys cannot be disciplined by their
own parents. . . .

James Fleming Jr.'s story hardly qualifies him for
the epithet "Son of Pain." . . .

And from a Maryland writer, several weeks earlier, to the
editor of the *Washington Post:*

To describe Christian Prince's trial as "a dramatic
clash between Ivy League privilege and inner city desperation" is irresponsible journalism at its worst. It is
obvious that [your reporter] does not know the difference between social injustice and cold-blooded murder. There is no clash. MURDER IS MURDER.

There were other such letters and enclosures. Some spoke
in support of the Brady Bill; others railed against the "un-
checked spread" of urban ghettos or the "handouts" that en-
able lives of "idleness and crime." One envelope, from all I
could tell, included no letter at all; only a quarter-folded cut-
out from the classified pages of the New Bern, North Carolina,
Sun Journal, April 7, 1991, with a single ad circled in pen:

RENT A HANDGUN
Most calibers available.
Only $4.00 plus ammo. B&R Guns
XXX-XXXX

There are two sides to every story.
"MURDER IS MURDER."
"These are *kids,* for Christ's sake."

The Prince family, like the letter writers, hated most of what the media wrote. It's not hard to see why.

"What kind of 'privilege' is it," Teddy Prince asked me, the night I met him and his family for the first time, "to come home to my 'suburban backyard swimming pool' and know that I'll never swim in it with my brother again?"

There are no answers to questions like this. You can only nod your head; you can only say you're sorry. The reporters behind those stories, if they were asked, might try to explain their vision of what they would call the "Big Picture." They would speak of the gap between rich and poor in America, and of the growing isolation of what Ken Auletta, in his 1983 book of the same name, tellingly labeled the "underclass."

If they were bold enough, they might point out that a murder such as Christian Prince's—as opposed to that of the black New Haven fifteen-year-old named Joseph Ford, who was shot to death with barely a peep of notice the day before—is the very sort of thing that forces white America to sit up and take notice of what is happening in our ghettos.

And they would be right. But the letter writers, and the Princes, would not be wrong.

It is beyond dispute to say that the murder of a son is a horrific thing to bear—and that to be labeled as "privileged" in its aftermath could seem, to the most insensate parent alive, an insolence of obscene proportions. It would be hard, also, to dispute the premise that "families in which 19-year-old unmarried women already have two children" are sometimes beyond help.

Neither side is wrong. But neither one either, in its remoteness from the other, can learn from its wisdoms or comprehend its pain. There is as much truth, and as much weight, in Merlin's anger—"You gonna look away and pretend like you don't see nothin' "—as there is in Sally Prince's inconsolable pain.

But it would be a cruelty—at least for now, and probably forever—to ask Sally to see it that way. As for Merlin, who has known more death and wastage in his twenty years than she will know in a lifetime, the loss of a son—of *ten* sons—couldn't begin to outweigh the unthinkable privilege that is hers: of moving through the world, day after day, utterly free from fear or want.

There have been moments, even since Christian's murder, when Sally Prince has had flashes of this. "We are so terribly aware," she told a *New York Times* reporter around the time of Dunc Fleming's first trial, "that these children have no chance in life."

But these moments, however they happened, have passed. Long since. The college philosophy major, the liberal, the mother who gave a day a week to poor families at an inner-city shelter, who once lobbied (successfully) for the integration of the Washington, D.C., Junior League; the moral exemplar to three children ("Do the right thing, be fair, be honest, love one another") who will tell you, proudly and no doubt truthfully: "There was never a bigoted remark made in this house"—all gone now. Invisible. "Poisoned," she tells me, with poison in her voice. Sally Prince is a hater today.

It goes beyond Dunc Fleming—the "evil monster" who (despite what any jury may say) pulled the trigger that took away her son. It goes beyond revenge. It is a hatred (though she will cringe when she reads these words) of all things black and poor. It is racist hatred. And, like the worst, the most pernicious of its type, it is rooted in the half-truths that can give ignorance the feel of gospel.

"I blame so many people. I blame the black leaders who tell these kids they're '*victims*'; I blame the media that keeps that [myth] alive. I blame the parents who perpetuate the same thing generation after generation—of children having children, without caring for them, without nurturing them, without providing in any way. . . .

"I probably blame his mother more than I blame him—for raising a *monster,* a child who was given no affection, no ambition, no compassion. A *subhuman being,* without the normal human instincts or beliefs.

"If the chain is ever going to stop, these kinds of people are going to have to stop producing children they don't know how to raise. . . ."

And it isn't only Sally. For Christian's brother Teddy, who was on antidepressants for months afterward and had nightmares for a year—he dreamed, recurrently, in vivid, playback detail, that it was *him* on the street that night—the notion of "justice" will be forever skewed.

"That lawyer who defended [Dunc Fleming], that guy who put those *liars* on the stand, he isn't worthy to be a member of the bar.

"When I heard the verdict, it just made me want to get sick. I was *at* that [first] trial; I heard those lies being told. . . .

"I've been through it so many times in my sleep—it always comes out the same. My brother gives him his wallet, does everything he asks—then the guy just puts a bullet through his heart. . . .

"But there was nothing I could do—*nothing.* I heard that verdict, I just smashed a glass against a tree. . . ."

There are other things Teddy Prince tells me. But he doesn't want to be quoted, he says. He knows it is probably groundless, "but I'm *scared,* I can't help it. If it could happen to him, I guess I think it could happen to me."

Even Ted Prince, the model of reason and forbearance, who has never in his life, he says, hated anyone—"I wouldn't know what it is to hate." Even he:

"[Since Christian died], sometimes when I see an idle black boy hanging out on the street, I feel an anger that I never knew before."

I have known racists. I have heard this kind of talk before: of child-mothers, the "victim myth," "these kinds of people"— but never from the likes of Ted or Sally Prince. Never from anyone whose cooking I have eaten, whose home and family and sorrows I have shared. Never from anyone I was as fond of, from anyone so like myself.

I want to argue. I want to tell them about Jim and Julia Fleming, and the hard work and the minimum-wage jobs, and Disney World, and the diabetes and heart attacks, and their plans for renewing their vows. I want to tell them: "No, you don't understand, they were a family once, just like yours. No, Sally, they tried—they tried their hearts out. You couldn't be more wrong."

But I know what will happen if I do. The same thing that happened with Christian's brother after I'd told him—stupidly, long before—something or other that Dunc had told to me. It was months before he could bring himself to talk with me again; "Just knowing you'd been in the same room with him," his sister told me at the time.

■ ■ ■

And so I say nothing. But what I go away thinking is this: That for one more white American family, black is bad, the root of evil, the root of violence, the cause of collapsed "family values" through which children are raised "without normal human instincts or beliefs."

For one more family, added to the millions already on board, there is now proof—in their case, *blood proof*—that the black ghetto boy is "subhuman," a "monster" who can pull the trigger of a gun and put a bullet through another boy's heart— a white boy's heart—without a tinge of pain or remorse, or so much as a backward look.

The black ghetto boy. The "idle black" on a street corner. Dunc Fleming with a twenty-two, out to get a "cracker." To the Prince family these days, they are one: one image, one menace, one single threat to life and safety, to the wholeness and happiness of a family of five.

For one more family, however much pain they have paid to earn their rage, the bridges between us have forever been cut.

19

Joe LaMotta was the kind of cop you'd call old-fashioned. He knew the aunts and mothers and brothers and teachers of the boys he arrested. He remembered names and faces. He pushed himself to try harder with the ones he thought had a chance—and lay awake nights, he remembers today, worrying about the others, the boys he calls the "doomed ones."

He is still that sort of man. But he isn't a cop anymore. He works in an office today: the district attorney's, on the second floor of the New Haven county court building, two floors below where Duncan Fleming was tried. His title is "victims' advocate," which means roughly what it says. He does what he can for the friends and families of those in the county who have been murdered or beaten or raped. He answers questions and provides referrals; he signs vouchers to get funerals paid for by the state—up to $2,400 is allowed. "A lot of these families," he explains, "haven't got the money to bury their kids."

On a small shelf alongside his desk is a row of books with the sorts of titles that go with the job: *How Do You Tell the Children?*, *Justice for Abused Children*, *No Time for Goodbyes*.

It's a thankless job, he says. It drains him. As he speaks of it, his shoulders sag and his voice goes flat with defeat.

"When I was a cop on the street, once in a while anyway, at least it *felt* like a win—a good arrest, a kid steered clear of something, the relationships you formed with the families and friends.

"But not anymore, not with this job. The closer I've gotten to the system, the more of the picture I've seen, the less hope I'm able to feel. . . .

"There's no end to it. You walk through the city pointing to places where your clients got killed. There's no elation in this job, no winners, no saving the day. There are only losers—it gets to you after a while."

Joe LaMotta is in his midthirties, a large man with plain features and close-cut dark hair. He is wearing a navy blue V-neck sweater over a shirt and tie. There is a directness about him, an artlessness almost, that makes the desk he sits at seem like some sort of useless toy.

He was on the street six years. He's been off it for two. As different as the jobs are, he says now, too many of the faces never change.

He tells the story of a boy named Daryl Brantley. He'd known him as a kid in Meriden: the city of sixty thousand, twenty miles or so north of New Haven, where LaMotta served his days as a cop. He'd pinched him once or twice: for shoplifting or vandalism, he can't recall just what—the sorts of small mischiefs some kids outgrow and others graduate from. He'd gotten to know the boy's mother; he'd come to think, over time, that Daryl might just make it, that he had a shot at coming through.

They'd lost touch. Six or eight years later, in his new job in the district attorney's office, he ran across him again, as the defendant in a pipe assault.

"I said to him then, 'Daryl, you stay with this kind of stuff, you're going to wind up dead or in jail.' He was dead a week later. The victim in the case, the kid he'd beaten with the pipe, he's been charged now himself with assault.

"Victim, defendant, defendant, victim—same names, same faces. It just goes 'round in circles. There's not much to tell between them, you might just as well flip a coin. . . ."

You've never heard or read of Daryl Brantley. You never will. He lived and died unremarkably, more or less seamlessly for a boy of his race and class. You take for granted, probably, that you know his story—and, in its essentials, more than likely you do. He was a poor black ghetto boy, a gang member. He may have sold drugs. His family, one way or another, was "broken." He had no ambition that you would call by that name, and next to no respect for life.

Ditto for his killer, and for the boy he beat with a pipe. The odds are good that at least one of them, like Daryl, is dead by this time, the other probably in jail. Dead or not, their existence isn't anything that you or I would call a life.

You would never, either, have heard of Duncan Fleming—if the boy he was charged with killing had been black and had gone to Hillhouse or Jackie Robinson instead of to Yale. They are much the same, these boys, in the hopeless, faceless anarchy that is the diet of their lives. Between victim and killer, as Joe LaMotta likes to say, it's usually no more than the flip of a coin.

But let's assume some things. Most of them are likely, none are far-fetched: All four boys, like Duncan, owned hundred-dollar gym shoes. Like Duncan and the pipe victim, all four had battle scars. All had had sex with more girls than they could remember or name. All belonged to a gang and could lay their hands—without hassle, within minutes—on a gun.

What would we say of such boys? We would say—we *do* say —that they are the cancer at our core. We would say, at least some of us, along with Sally Prince, that they are monsters, that their mothers and fathers had no business conceiving them, that anarchy begins in the home. We would say, as our president has said more than once—a caring president, as presidents go—that they reflect the "great crisis of spirit" in our cities, that they are the surest sign we can point to that our nation is ill. And we, like him, would call for more police. And we would not be wrong.

But what do these boys call themselves? Or each other? What do their girlfriends say? Or their fathers or mothers, or their MTV icons, or any of the voices that, from day to day, inform their lives?

They call themselves "niggers"—an inversion of the most vicious racial slur of our time. Ask them what it means, and they'll tell you: a second inversion, this one the highest, most telling praise of all. It means, they say, that they are *"ba-aaad."*

"Nigger" as hero. Bad as good. A jail term or bullet wound as a diploma of worth. Everything is reversed in this world:

symbols, values, vernacular. Upside down. The whole house of cards, as most of us know it, has been inverted—deliberately, defiantly—by an entire subculture, millions strong, who live in our cities and murder each other, by the thousands, every year.

They see whites as the enemy. They will tell you so to your face. Yet it is blacks—fellow "niggers"—that they gun for and kill. They are outnumbered, outeducated, impoverished, isolated, and despised. Without hope of reversal. And so, in their impotence—like leaderless, ragtag guerrillas in search of a cause—they make war among themselves. Over drug turfs or gold chains or Air Jordans—but their real fight is with the world.

"Being a teenager these days is *brutal,*" Lisa Sullivan, a black New Haven activist, told *The New Yorker*'s William Finnegan three years ago. "It's much worse than it was in the forties, when people were afraid of the Klan, of being called 'nigger,' of having someone spit on them. These kids [today] know that the whole society hates who they are. And they can't *help* who they are. Why do you think their favorite band calls itself Public Enemy Number One?"

But as "niggers," are they failures? Or even just as kids—by the standards of children anywhere, white or black? Could we say, with any real fairness, that these are boys who don't conform, who don't achieve?

They drop out of school by the hundreds of thousands. But school, in the ghetto, is no mark of worth. They live, many of them, outside the law. But what meaning has law to a boy whose father may be absent, whose pop heroes make vermin of police, and half of whose friends are dead or in jail?

They find their roots in "posses," which the rest of us call gangs. "But what you call a gang," Tanya Fleming told me one day, "I call just having friends."

They measure themselves, like boys anywhere, by the symbols and totems that society prescribes. Gold and silver, a Raiders warm-up jacket, a pair of gym shoes with the name or image of an NBA star. They haunt the malls and arcades of every downtown. They go to movies and pick up girls, and have crude sex in the backs of cars. They watch TV fifty hours a week—and covet the products that are touted by idols they would trade their eyeteeth to be.

They are kids. Conformists, consumers, American boys. They long, as fervently as your kid or mine, to be accepted, to be "where it's at," to belong.

But they're not. They never have been. They are outcasts: social pariahs at whose door is laid much of the hatred and meanness that makes our country ill. And until recently—until the explosion of cocaine in our cities put obscene dollars within reach of any boy willing to risk his freedom and his life —there seemed no recourse, no route to brightness or hope.

They would live their lives, as they viewed it, much as they had watched their fathers live theirs. They would leave school too early, work at jobs that paid as little as they asked, then quit and go on welfare, and smoke reefer on street corners with other black boys as angry and hopeless as they. They would steal, and fight, and drink too much and marry too young, then father children they had neither the means nor the will to raise.

The best of them, like Jim Fleming, would find jobs worth holding—then work for years for the dignity of a superintendent's badge and the small pleasures of a trip to Disney World. But even Jim Fleming, for all his twenty-three years of hopeful grinding, is a castoff today: a one-eyed, one-legged human shadow with two daughters on welfare and nothing to show for his days.

This, except for the lucky ones—the brains and the athletes, and the one in ten whose grit brought them through—was the long and short of it: the birthright of being black and city pent and poor.

Then came cocaine. And how quickly, how rapaciously—how like young men anywhere who dream of proving themselves—these boys attacked their chance.

Soundless, vibrating beepers that warn of a cop's approach. Walkie-talkies that connect dealers a neighborhood apart. Corner-by-corner watch systems, code names, hierarchies, nine-year-old decoys who signal when a rival is near.

It is not uncommon, as any public defender will tell you, for a boy to buy his mother's house. Some launder money through the purchase of jewelry; others hide their incomes behind settlements from police brutality suits. At least one midlevel dealer, a Hartford sixteen-year-old on trial for assault, arrived at the courthouse in a stretch limo with a chauffeur at the wheel and a blue-and-gold bumper sticker in back: "I Support the PBA."

"These kids," says Joe LaMotta, "they know exactly what they're doing, and exactly what they want. They've been out there awhile. As salesmen, they're as good as it gets. They're smart; they're calculating; they're entrepreneurs—you couldn't call them anything less."

The same, he says, holds true in the courtroom. "They know just what you want to hear. They can play the victim's game. You've got to watch out, you've got to be real careful, what you buy from these guys. . . ."

■ ■ ■

Christian Prince, a mediocre schoolboy athlete, was all-American at seventeen. A "disappointing" sixth-grade student, he found his way to Yale. An eight-year-old so retiring he could barely meet the eyes of a family friend, ten years later he was vice president of his school.

And Dunc Fleming. By his father's admission, "never much of a student"—though he stayed in school in a culture where schooling doesn't count for much. As an athlete, which never counted either (even when there were fields without guns nearby), he barely even tried.

But, he tells me, from behind his side of the table in the prison's visiting room—and there is pride, I can see, in the telling of it: "I'm still here, ain't I? You be lookin' at me, you be talkin' to me right now. Lotta people from 'round my way, they be *underground,* they be dead and gone by now. . . ."

And he has lots of sneakers. And he's had his share of girls. And the bullet wound he carries like a soldier wears his stripes.

As for money or guns, or protection from the gang crosstown, or whatever else it takes: "I need it, I get it. Like I told you, we all be family, man. . . ."

Christian Prince could have been Sam Douglas: my only son, my only child. He would be "underground" nearly three years by now. And I would be a broken father consumed, no doubt, by hate. It would be anathema to me, a vulgarity—as it is, so viscerally, to the Princes today—to hear him contrasted to the boy who took his life.

But the contrasts, and parallels, are too clear to deny. And to remain blind to them—to dismiss these boys as monsters, to mask our rage and impotence behind calls for less guns or more police—is to ensure, in perpetuity, that there will be more rage, more separateness, and more deaths.

Christian Prince's lacrosse stick, in every way but literally, was Dunc Fleming's twenty-two. Christian's "ferociousness" on the playing field was Dunc's grit in staying alive. The one's posse was the other's Yale. Both boys, by the standards and opportunities of their worlds, were survivors. One prevailed; the other merely got by. But getting by, on the streets of New Haven's inner city, is a prevailing of its own.

To be sure, there are boys from the Newhallville ghetto who go on to lives as rich and worthy as Christian Prince's would have been. But they are few—as few perhaps as there are Yale graduates who die destitute or fugitive or in jail. And to ask of these young black boys (to ask of any boys anywhere) that they accept, without rage or rancor, the realistic limits of a law-abiding ghetto boy's dreams—to be a dishwasher or line worker or superintendent or cook—is to ask, it would seem, far too much.

They have *not* accepted. Nor would your son or mine. For years, for generations, they have raged and demonstrated, and defied the law in large ways and small, and formed street gangs with nothing—until recently—but invisible lines to protect.

Most, in the end, have succumbed: to welfare or alcoholism, or the despised, dead-ended drudgery of their fathers' lives and ways. They lived and worked and died—as Jim Fleming will, and a million others have before—with anger and bitterness, and shriveled, thwarted hopes.

But no longer. Today they can say, with swagger if not with pride, that they are "humpin' for dollars," that the white world has nothing on them. They can say, with some truth, that they have freedom—because in the ghetto, as any child or adult will tell you, freedom and dollars are the same.

They will tell you now, too—as Merlin told me that morning in the living room of the Flemings' home—that there is a purpose to their days: "I got me a job just like you, man. Nine, ten in the morning, troop sometimes till one at night. I'm on the move, man, on my feet twelve, thirteen hours a day. There ain't nobody can't say I don't *earn* that money, I'm sayin'?"

Between 1986 and early 1990, literally thousands of New Haven boys "got down." Some dropped out of school to do it; by 1988, the city's drop-out rate was the highest in the state. Others left jobs washing dishes or pumping gas—from four dollars an hour to four hundred dollars a day.

Crime went through the roof. In the eight years prior to early 1987, a public defender was quoted as saying, he could recall only a single juvenile being arrested for drugs. By mid-1990, he had more than fifty cases on the books. Not one of his clients was over fifteen.

Six months before he told this to a reporter, the city's murder rate had hit an all-time high. Eighty-five percent of the victims were black.

If such figures don't define anarchy, I can't conceive of what would.

20

It's common today to hear talk of the "breakdown of family values." Of parents no longer able to control or set examples for their kids. And no doubt there is some truth in this. We are a more fragmented, more alienated people than we were ten or twenty years ago.

"There are days, I swear," says Joe LaMotta, "when I feel like I'm just shoveling sand. . . . The churches have lost their younger members; family values are eroding; the schools can't keep the kids. The whole transmission of values—it just seems to have broken down."

But Jim and Julia Fleming, for all the hardships that beset them, never once forsook their kids. The examples they set—of churchgoing, and daily work, and family time—were rooted early and consistently, and (from all I can tell) very well. They were good parents, within their means—or tried their best to be.

But there were other examples set too, to nobody's credit or fault: that faith in God, at least for poor folk, is rarely rewarded; that a lifetime of work gets you nothing but a paycheck that is meager to begin with and ends, with no recourse but handouts, when you can no longer carry the load; that for every family trip to Disney World, there is a week or a month of overheard squabbles over bills that can't be paid.

So Dunc Fleming, like millions of other young black boys from Newhallville to Watts, made his family on the street. He joined a posse, got shot through the legs, saw a score of friends buried, and did or didn't sell drugs.

But whether he did or didn't, there was wealth enough to go around. And guns enough. He was a "brother" now among brothers, who would risk their lives for him. There was pride in that. (Even today, more than two years behind bars, it is the proudest thing he knows.) And if life was cheap—and it was—it had never, to begin with, been dear.

Jim and Julia Fleming, as I have come to know them—and to know the street world of Dunc's choosing, which they did their best to combat—were helpless to prevent what may or may not have happened that February night. They set curfews; they made it their business to know their son's friends; they lectured endlessly about drugs. Against tall odds, and despite his own hardships, Jim Fleming's insistence had kept his boy in school.

But their efforts were doomed before they started—as they must have sensed long before that night. The values and examples of a parent, in the eyes of any boy old enough to judge, cannot help but be measured against the promise they hold.

"Jewelry, gold, clothes—that's what [these kids] dream of," Jim Fleming told *The New York Times* the week after his son's first trial. "Not just James. Any [of these kids] is fascinated by big money.

"I'd say to him, 'James you have to finish school, to get an education, you can't just start at the top.' I'd try to instill in him that he had to take care of himself, because no one else would. . . ."

Christian Prince had looked at his father and seen a man as blessed as he was good. Successful, healthy, wealthy, contented, and fulfilled. Any rebellions that might be expected from the son of such a father would not have taken him far from the fold.

But there are no jobs, no values, no promises or rewards that can compete, for any son of Jim Fleming, with the seductions of the street. If such a boy is to find deliverance—and there are some, though far too few, who do—the messages that bring it are not apt to begin in the home.

"You can't imagine the pain of some of these parents," Joe LaMotta tells me. His head is lowered and shaking, and his hands are balled into fists. "They all have the same questions, the same impotence—'What could I have done different? Where did we go wrong?' "

(I think, as he speaks, of Julia Fleming, in her living room not three weeks before: "I tried my best, did everything I knew how. But look at where it's got me—James is in jail, and I ain't even fifty yet and a grandmother to three little kids. I musta went wrong somewhere, but as God is my witness I surely don't know where.")

"And you have to tell them," says LaMotta, "and it's so awfully, awfully hard—'Your kid isn't going to grow up the way you did, never mind better. You can't help him, he's past you. Your values don't apply on the street. . . .'"

He stops and leans forward. His arms fly from his sides like wings.

"But who am I to tell them *anything*—much less about life on the street?

"'You don't live where I live'—I hear that a lot from these families. 'You don't sleep where I sleep, or go to school with my baby brother, or hear what I hear at night. So who are *you* to judge?'

"And they're right, you know. They couldn't be more right. What can I say that's going to mean anything to these people? I've never lived in the ghetto. I don't even live in this town. . . ."

Joe LaMotta is an "advocate." A part of his job is to understand pain. But he is also an ex-cop. He has made arrests. He has locked handcuffs on the wrists of some of the same boys whose mothers he now gives checks to help bury. He would do it again if need be.

He wants me to know this. He wants me to understand that his two worlds are one—and that their truths are not as simple as he fears I might try to make them seem.

He has seen too many reporters and writers (he has told me this already several times), too many people with jobs and intentions like my own, arrive and ask questions, and attend trials and hold interviews with the families he sees—then leave and write the stories that were written in their heads before they came.

"Labels are easy," he says to me now. "If it's labels you came for, you came to the wrong man."

He tells me this story about labels, and about the damage they can do: In 1974, a black boy named Melvin Jones shot and killed a white boy named Gary Stein—the last time, before Christian Prince, that a Yale student had been murdered in New Haven. Jones was convicted and imprisoned, then released fifteen years later, in the fall of 1989. Within six months, he had killed again. This time, though, his victim was a street kid. Again he was convicted. Joe LaMotta was at the trial.

"There was this reporter there [for the *Hartford Courant*, the largest paper in the state]; she was covering the case. And everyday, she'd come into the courtroom and head right for the family of Melvin Jones. She'd hug them; she'd sit with them; they'd talk together on breaks—I never saw her go near the dead kid's family. There wasn't much doubt where her sympathies lay."

(Jones, a grown man by then, had declined the service of lawyers and elected to defend himself. For that reason as much as any other, he was a hero to many. It was a widely covered case.)

"Then her story came out in the paper. And sure enough. The dead boy, it said, had been a *'drug addict'*—there wasn't a shred of evidence to support that claim. It was a label, that's all, an easy answer. It fit the stereotype. . . .

"I *saw* that family's pain. It was incredible. It was like their boy had died twice.

"But there wasn't a thing they could do about it. They would live with that label the rest of their lives."

■ ■ ■

We have spent ninety minutes together, perhaps more. For nearly all of this time, Joe LaMotta has been speaking as the "advocate" he is: of the pain and rage and impotence of ghetto families, the breakdown of values, the suffering he sees every day. "The ghetto saps your energy"—it is where my notes have stopped.

Abruptly, almost awkwardly, he shifts. His voice picks up energy; there is a new urgency to his tone. He is all cop now. It is as though somehow—for the moment—he's forgotten that he's ever been anything else.

"Listen. The bottom line is *responsibility*. The acceptance of responsibility. There's no substitute for that. It's easy to feel sorry for these people; it's easy to get lost behind all these images and labels, behind all the 'victim' talk. We live in a victims' society today.

"But if Dunc Fleming killed Christian Prince, then he's got to pay for it. He's got to go to jail. In the end, it comes down to that. . . ."

So then what are your hopes for the future? I ask him. What keeps you on the job? If the street, and what comes with it, is the strongest lure these kids know; if you have little or nothing to say to these families that will hold meaning in their world—and the final answer is an eye for an eye—then what's the use of advocates? Why not just put a cop on every block?

He smiles. It is a wry smile, and a very small one, but a smile nonetheless. The first, perhaps, I've seen from him since we introduced ourselves.

"Some of these kids *do* survive. Some of them make it out. You've just got to try and save the ones you can. . . ."

21

There may be no one in New Haven, white or black, who is held in more reverence by black boys on the street—or offers them more hope—than the man who calls himself Scott X.

He is in his early thirties: a Black Muslim, a follower of Louis Farrakhan and the teachings of Elijah Muhammad. Until two or three years ago, he owned and ran a lunch counter, called Shabazz, on the fringe of the Newhallville ghetto, in which he sometimes gave jobs to troubled black youth.

But that was no more than a sideline. Scott X is an evangelist. A politician without an office, an activist and organizer, a missionary for his cause. Part hero, part mentor, to New Haven's young blacks.

More than once, he has mediated turf wars between rival

posses that more than likely would have cost lives. In 1989, it is widely agreed, he was a major force behind the election of the city's first black mayor—John Daniels—who served one term and was gone.

Since then, he's launched "Elm City Nation," which—on a shoestring, largely through free ads in black papers and posters tacked up all over town—sponsors plays and ball games and neighborhood meetings widely attended by New Haven's young blacks. His most recent creation, "Black Expo," is a yearly showcase of the products and talents of the best of the city's black half: artists, musicians, small businesspeople, cooks and clothiers and kids. On its maiden outing, in the New Haven armory in the spring of 1993, it drew a one-day crowd of close to five thousand—a number they're aiming to double next time out.

Through these means, and less public ones (there's no telling the number of troubled young blacks who've come to Scott X for help), he has steered uncountable boys away from the lures of lives on the street. He has been, without question, a force for great good.

I've never met this man. The closest we got was a phone call, placed from a public booth less than a mile from his home. I told him who I was and why I was calling. "I've heard a lot about you; I'd like an hour of your time" was the gist of what I said.

He was civil, though barely. But I never even got close:

"I've got nothing to say to you. What's your book going to do besides make you lots of money? I've read those kinds of books before. You got anything new to say about *us?*"

I tried. He listened briefly. There was some line about "white oppressors" (that's all I managed to get down). Then the end came very fast:

"We've got nothing to talk about, Mister Douglas"—and the connection between us went dead.

It was the same response, almost word for word, that he'd offered *The New Yorker*'s William Finnegan three years before. Scott X, as a matter of personal policy, doesn't talk to white reporters.

But Finnegan, I guess, was more persistent, or more persuasive, than I. Or maybe Scott X has just hardened over time. However it happened, the two of them met at least twice face-to-face. Their second meeting, from all I can gather, was mostly about Scott's case against whites.

"Your people have kept my people in chains for four hundred years. We don't owe you *anything*. You say you're interested in the troubles of the black community. We say you are *responsible* for those troubles. You say you can't keep the drugs from coming in. We don't believe that. You can throw a satellite up to Neptune, but you can't control the borders of your own country?

"We are about helping the black community, and I can't see how anything you write is going to help us. How many black readers does your magazine have?"

Scott X is a fundamentalist. Fundamentalists believe, more or less by definition, in simple, literal answers to often complex things. The Bad Guy and the Good Guy. Us against Them. The Bible or Koran as scripture-truth.

I admire the mission of Scott X and can be thankful for the good it has done. But I can't help but feel, despite this, that the influence of such a man is a dangerous thing. It divides us. It contributes to separateness, which contributes to envy, which contributes—over time, and with inequality to feed it—inevitably, to hate.

You can't go anywhere in New Haven's black ghettos, or in the ghettos of any city you or I could name, without hearing the message of white against black. It is in Merlin's talk of "racial shit" ("Party in a black neighborhood? Police go, 'fuck it, let 'em kill themselves' "), and Dunc's bitterness at the white-skinned, four-time arsonist who walked out of court ("It's all a setup, man"). Even Julia Fleming, who didn't grow up around hate: "The black man, he be workin' for the white man. It be the *white* man who be bringin' in these drugs—these drugs that's killin' our kids. But what you gonna do? It's a white man's world out there."

These people—or at least the young among them—have no perspective to speak of on the oppression of their race. To most, Malcolm X is a movie; Medgar Evers or Rosa Parks would draw blank stares. Except for the handful of activists who work with Scott X, not one in twenty could tell you a thing about Nat Turner or Harriet Tubman or Ralph Abernathy, or what happened in Selma in 1965.

They know only that they are poor—and that whites are somehow to blame. And that to make As in school is to risk the charge of "acting white." They couldn't tell you, in terms any more precise than Julia Fleming's, why any of this is true. It simply is. It has never, in their memories, been any other way.

It's not hard to see why. Slavery, which began all this thinking, is a bitter legacy, from whichever side you view it: ownership as a birthright, oppression as a condition of birth. And since then: Reconstruction, carpetbaggers, the Negro as "enfranchised," Uncle Tom, the KKK, George Wallace and Bull

Durham, Medgar Evers and Malcolm X—then the Supreme Court and "affirmative action" as mirrors of our intent.

All the distortions and reversals and dislocations that come of upheaval, of "reconstructing," of trying to change—against our instincts, and much of our history—the way we think and feel.

Yet still we whites are richer—by miles. And have more access, more influence, more jobs outside McDonald's, more time to choose to waste. Not to mention more votes. And still we have our David Dukes—and the hundreds of thousands who vote for them, and the millions more who would if they could.

We are nowhere near equal. It will be decades, if ever—in Julia Fleming's terms—before, in our country, it's anything other than a "white man's world out there."

But the *real* issue—at least for Dunc and Merlin, and for several million other ghetto-bound American youths—has nothing to do with race. Or with poverty or crime. Or values, or drugs, or broken families, or even hate. Just as pneumonia, really, has nothing to do with AIDS—though it is often, in coroners' terms, the reported cause of death.

The real issue, today, is nothingness. Vacantness. A hole in the blanket where there ought to be wool. A reason to play football, or make As, or win a girl's heart (or body) without having to buy it with money it took nothing to make. A reason to live, and to *keep* living. To believe in tomorrow. To care about life.

A reason not to be a "nigger"—not to want to call yourself by some name that was invented, centuries ago, by those to whom you were chattel: to be bought and sold and exploited and raped, then hung by the neck (a century later, when they couldn't own you anymore) if you dared even to covet one of theirs.

A reason to want to be a part—a working part, however distinct—of a people and a system who have viewed you (progressively) as property, then problem, then (reluctantly) as a bill to be paid.

Your people have kept my people in chains for four hundred years. . . ."

"You gonna . . . look away and pretend like you don't see nothin', you don't see that poor nigger sittin' there. . . ."

These are the voices of a people, not at the *bottom* of society ("the lower class")—as we have so long, and so glibly, allowed ourselves to believe—but *outside* it, literally, with a society and a system of their own.

For all of their numbers, and their swagger, and their sneakers-driven consumer ways, these are a people who have given up. Dropped out. Isolated themselves, in clusters of tens or hundreds of thousands, in ghettos at the centers of our cities —from where they have severed, with appalling completeness, most of the bridges and values (laws, schools, safety nets, the system as a whole) upon which our society, at least in theory, is built.

Close to 60 percent of all our black families—the number, by now, may be higher—make their homes in the inner city. The figure for whites is roughly 25 percent. (It is common, among black leaders especially, to refer to this as the "warehousing" of their race.)

Family income for the poorest fifth of black families, in 1991, was just over forty percent of the comparable figure for poor whites. Roughly one white person of every ten lived below the poverty line; among blacks, nearly one in three.

Other numbers reflect values almost more cultural than economic: In 1986, 5,877 babies were born in the United States to black girls fourteen years old or younger. For whites (who comprise about 80 percent of our population), the number was 4,077.

Such gulfs carry over to families: 42 percent of all black ones, in 1988, were headed by a single woman. White single women headed roughly one in eight.

And crime. In 1988, according to the FBI's *Uniform Crime Reports,* 16,090 suspects were arrested for murder. Of these, 8,603—roughly 53 percent—were black. For robbery arrests, the gap was wider: 62 percent—a rate, in proportion to population, more than ten times that of whites.

This is not "falling through the cracks," as our social scientists like to say. It is anarchy. A breakdown of *everything*—social, cultural, moral, familial—that we would define as "civilized." It is *two societies*—not at war, not even just separate, but totally (and increasingly) estranged. Irrelevant, one to the other. Yet at the same time both hated and feared.

"A vast vacuum"—our president has called it (though it is unclear that he understands just how vast, or what the solutions might be)—"which has been filled by violence and drugs and gangs. So I ask you to remember that, even as we say no to crime, we must give people, especially our young people, something to say yes to."

And there's more to chart it by than just crime or poverty or early teen mothers. These are only the more ballyhooed signs.

The others are less stark but more sinister. In many ways, they tell the fuller tale.

Ghetto poor people—especially blacks—are turning off their phones. Between 1988 and 1992, according to an FCC study of six cities, the number of phoneless households increased in five of them. In Boston, more than a fourth of poor black and Hispanic households are now without telephones. Among whites in the same income range, the figure is barely 10 percent.

They're not voting, either. In the 1992 elections, although voter turnout in general hit a twenty-four-year high (55.9 percent), only 26 percent of the nation's poorest voters went to the polls—the lowest figure in at least ten years.

A lot of them aren't even bothering to send their kids to school. Although this trend may be harder to track (most cities reportedly, in an effort to save dollars, have done away with their truancy teams), it's becoming more visible to those who pay attention to such things.

"You find seven-, eight-, nine-, and ten-year-olds who've never been to school," a Boston housing official told the *Boston Globe* in the winter of 1993–94. "You find them all over the place."

The *Globe,* in a striking three-part series by reporter Peter S. Canellos in early February 1994, tracked the drift toward isolation among the poorest of our poor. A vastly disproportionate segment of these people are black. Nearly all make their homes in the cities:

> They are the cast-offs and drop-outs who were left out of the boom of the '80s, and who are living [today] in a world apart. . . . And in the vacuum in which they live, it's unclear whether society holds any claims on them, or power to censure. . . .

[Their] existence is a standing rebuke to such ever-green American maxims as voting can empower people; all able-bodied people can find jobs; and every generation cherishes giving education opportunities to the next. . . .

In Suffolk County, which includes Boston, 1,896 cases were dismissed in 1992 and the first nine months of 1993, because victims or witnesses failed to show up. . . .

The primary reason for [their] disappearing is fear—a sense that the criminal justice system cannot protect people from gangs or stalkers.

The second reason . . . is more frightening. Without jobs to bring them into contact with people, or meaningful social ties, members of the outer class aren't accustomed to talking to officials. They believe the system is their enemy. They don't see it as their duty to help police. . . .

"The whole issue is *separateness*," says Tim Shriver, the social development supervisor of New Haven's school system. "Highways, suburbs, TV, burglar alarms—there's no sense of a shared future; we're growing farther apart every day."

If there is any hope, Shriver tells me—from across the table of a New Haven coffee shop on an early winter morning in 1993—it lies with the schools.

"Everything else has collapsed around these kids—families, churches, peer groups, everything. But you can't address this just by adding more social workers, more judges, more police. That's crazy. You've got to try to create an institution that supports the families, that supports the kids, that puts opportunities within their reach. . . .

"The only one that still has the capacity to play that role is the school. But we've got to change it—to expand it way beyond what it is. Our schools simply have to grow up. . . .

"We've got to mold them into community-centered institutions—places that stay open late, that offer mentor relations, dialogue, problem-solving groups, places these kids can go and be heard. . . ."

He tells me about a "teen leadership" group he runs. They've been meeting weekly now for close to seven years.

"It's just a group of guys in high school. We just talk, do projects, go to basketball games—no Boy Scout stuff, no uniforms or field trips, none of that bullshit. We just *get together*.

"And the responses—you wouldn't believe it. It's like, 'Yeah, wow, okay—it's safe to say things here like, I'm having problems with my girlfriend, or I'm having problems at home. . . .'

"All you give them is support, an ear. The sense that nobody's judging them, that's there's no reason to have to be cool.

"I swear, you'd think you just delivered manna from heaven."

Tim Shriver doesn't have much patience with what he calls the "America, You Suck" line of thought. He's tired, he says, of most of what he reads in the papers, and of the "guilt-trip books" that contrast the "sewage-seeping hallways" of inner-city schools with the playing fields and classrooms of their suburbs ten minutes away.

"That's crap—that won't accomplish a thing. People made their peace with that a long time ago. 'Look,' they'll tell you, 'I got guilty twenty years ago, and it didn't do any good. So, you want me to feel guilty again?'

"As a society, we haven't done *anything*. Everybody goes around throwing up their hands—'We've tried this, we've tried that'—that's bullshit. We haven't done anything. At least nothing that's going to make any difference, that's going to do any good. . . .

"Words, messages, they don't change a thing—any more than they do with kids. *Relationships* change kids—the grandmother, the doctor who takes an interest, the sweet old lady next door. . . .

"We have to find ways to interact. People have to learn to live together, to see together—not in a contrived way, not because I set up some sort of program that does it, just because it happens.

"If we don't provide these kids with some opportunities—to see the world, to identify with significant people, to address their rage, the disarray in their families—then there's no reason—no *good* reason—for them not to do anything.

"As it is now, nobody seems to give a shit whether anything's right or wrong. You might as well do wrong as right. Nobody cares anyway. It doesn't seem to carry much weight either way. . . ."

The aimless rage of [criminals] strikes at society in the form of shocking, brutal, and random acts of violence [Peter Canellos wrote in the *Globe*]. Each city has its own paradigmatic crime, its own moment when the greater community suddenly realizes that something horrible and strange is happening in the fissures of society.

In Boston [in 1993] it was when a jazz musician sitting in a chicken restaurant was set upon and clubbed to death with a box radio. . . .

In New Haven, Connecticut, in February of 1991—whoever the killer and whatever the details (and neither, with any certainty, will probably ever be known)—it was when a nineteen-year-old Yale student with a golden future and no real arguments with the world was shot through the heart for the simple reason that, in the eyes of whoever pulled the trigger, it was utterly unimportant whether he lived, or was maimed forever, or died.

22

"Society better do something. It's out of control. . . ."

Susan Storey sits next to me, on one side of an oval-shaped table in the "conference room" of the Hartford Public Defender's Office. She puts me in mind of a greyhound: thin and sleek, and oddly wonderful to look at, but with a tautness about her, a torturedness almost, that makes her seem ready to spring.

(It is an intentness I've grown used to. I've seen it by now in the faces and movements of a dozen or more men and women I've met with, those whose work takes them daily into the lives —the homes or streets or courtrooms—of the hopeless poor. It arises, or seems to, out of a years-long accretion of stifled rage.)

Susan Storey is white and perhaps thirty-five. As is her partner, Ellen Knight, the social anthropologist who sits across the table from us now, but spends the bulk of her workdays in the homes of the suspects her lawyer-colleagues defend—because, as she puts it: "You've got to go back to the beginning with these people to have any hope of getting the truth."

Both women ooze anger. Both talk so fast, often concurrently—or barely consecutively, the one finishing the other's last thought—it is hard (I'll learn later in reviewing my notes) to keep straight just who said what. Both, like Joe LaMotta, have their share of horror stories, which they tell with such fierceness, almost muttering sometimes, I have to fight the urge to tell them that I am overloaded, that I have heard enough.

The violence, the squalor, the incest, the bite marks on forearms and thighs. Five-year-olds as sexual objects; lead poisoning, AIDS, booze, crack babies, fetal alcohol syndrome; the heatless, phoneless, food-rotting, roach-filled homes. The "little friend" who shot his sister "by accident"; the teenage mother with a butter knife—belonging to her boyfriend, known as "Daddy" to her kids—embedded in her head.

The system, the "burnout," the indifferent juries, the plea-bargained killings (nearly all, they say, are black-on-black), the jailhouse snitches, the Reagan cutbacks that "hung these kids out to rot" . . .

(All this—*just* this—is more than ninety minutes of our time. Close to two full cassettes, seventeen pages on a five-by-eight legal pad.)

Both women, at different times, describe it all as "hopeless." Yet both insist they love their jobs.

"I wouldn't want to do anything else in the world," Storey

tells me at one point. "I give *good law*"—and here she allows herself a little smirk. "It's about the best these kids can hope to get."

At the core of both women's commitment (and they are as committed as any two people I've known) is the notion that, for ghetto children, the ghetto itself is oppression enough to, if not justify, at least "mitigate" the guilt behind almost any crime.

Unlike Joe LaMotta (or Ted or Sally Prince, or most of the rest of us probably), they would not tell you that "responsibility" is any sort of bottom line—except legally, and they'd change *that* if they could. The bottom line, for these two, is that the children they work for are already living a fate far worse than any jail.

"Self-defense should be redefined for a kid from the ghetto," says Storey. "Whether anyone is holding a gun to their head or not, they live in immediate danger every day."

The danger they speak of is not only—not even mostly—physical. This becomes clearer as we talk.

"We're dealing with a whole different agenda here," Ellen Knight says now. "A whole different way of thinking. It's hard for you or I to comprehend.

"Issues like right and wrong, good and bad? They're not even on the *table*. . . .

"You try to talk to these kids about pain, deprivation—about their fears that their mother will get stabbed by her boyfriend or their best friend might get shot? They just look at you funny—that stuff's not even on the surface enough for them to *feel* anymore. . . ."

(Her words bring to mind Tanya Fleming: "Don't go to funerals no more. Not since Taz. . . . When he died, Dunc and me, we cried our eyes out behind the building, cried till there was no more cryin' to do.")

"There's nothing to these people's lives. *Nothing.* No sense of reward, no sense of control. Their families have no money; they have limited vocabularies, limited social skills; their dealings with the outside world are about as narrow as it gets. All there is is the street. And making it through the day.

"You live like that for long enough, you know what happens? It would happen to any of us. After a while your whole thought process just cuts out everyone else. You go back to thinking like a child—'Nothing else matters, it's just me against the world.'

"That's a lot of the reason, I think, why it's so easy to pull the trigger. . . ."

Susan Storey recounts a scene she has witnessed, she says, within the last seven days. It's apparently a common one.

"Some guy will walk in here, some guy [whose defense] is assigned to this office—he'll walk up to the receptionist out front, who's probably never seen him in her life.

" '*When's my case?*' he'll ask her. No name, no details, no [docket number], nothing. Just 'When's my case?'

"*Imagine* that—that level of insulation, of egocentricity, of being so cut off and alone it wouldn't occur to you to tell a stranger your name. . . ."

I ask them their hopes—though they have told me already they have none. (It has become my habit by now, the question I end with. The answers, as a rule, are pretty bleak.)

"You mean the *rewards?*" Ellen Knight asks me back. The cynicism in her voice is as brittle as a frozen stick. "You mean the credit we get—*if* we get it—for a 'job well done'?"

That's a start, I answer—though it's nowhere near what I'd had in mind.

"Applause," one of them answers. (My sense is she means this literally: I picture a courtroom full of clapping, hooting blacks.) "You get applause from a family for 'Life Without Parole,' for keeping their kid off Death Row."

(Connecticut, though it rarely applies it, is one of thirty-odd states that carry the death penalty for so-called capital crimes. As of late 1992, according to the Bureau of Justice, four Connecticut prisoners were inmates on Death Row.)

But beyond this?—I try again. Is gun control the answer? If you took drugs off the streets, would that keep crime at bay?

"Everything now, one way or another, is drug related," Ellen Knight answers, almost without drawing a breath. "You get drugs out of the picture, at least you'd be addressing the problem—but 'addressing' it is about as far as it goes. . . ."

As for guns, she says, just as quickly: "There's *way* too much anger out there. You take guns out of the equation? There's not a question in my mind—they'd use knives."

We are winding up. I've closed my notebook; my recorder is turned off. One of the two women (I honestly forget which) is telling me some very funny story about her husband (or someone's husband) burning his TV dinner in the microwave in protest for having to eat Lean Cuisine with only the dog as company ten or twelve worknights in a row.

Then, suddenly, as though a switch has been flipped—or was never off to begin with—Susan Storey turns back on. We have been together since two-thirty. It's now after six.

"You know what's really *strange?*"—she picks up as seam-

lessly as if the microwave story were about to get some new
twist. "At least I used to think it was strange. Now I just think
it's really, really sad. . . .

"These people I defend? They actually *enjoy* it. The whole
process—it actually makes them feel *good*.

"It's like, for the first time in their lives, everything is so
orderly, so simple. They know what's expected of them; they
know what they're going to be doing all day.

"They wear a suit; they wear a tie. They look good. There's
a sense of order, for better or worse. They get a lot of attention;
there's a purpose to their lives. A sense, at least for that day
[or week] they spend in court, that *somebody cares*. . . .

"I just look at them sometimes, and I think—how pathetic,
how incredibly sad. To be that desperate for dignity, to need it
so badly you can actually *enjoy* being on trial for your
life. . . ."

I am at the door now. My coat is in my hand. It is close to
seven—though neither woman, I can plainly see, is anywhere
near ready to call it a day. They stand in the hallway, saying
their goodbyes, as ready to return to their offices as I am to eat
a meal.

"I guess we've made it all sound pretty futile," Susan Storey
says now. She is smiling, or trying to. She seems, for the first
time in more than four hours, almost relaxed. An attractive
woman, with gentle eyes.

"You're probably wondering why we even bother to come in
to work every day."

I tell her I've asked myself that question lately about a lot of
people I've met.

"Well, maybe there's more hope than we realize. You're

writing this book, aren't you? Somebody out there is paying you to get it in print. That says something, I guess. . . .

"Because as it is now—and this is all it comes down to in the end—as it is now, *nobody really cares. . . .*"

She is winding up again. The tautness is back, and the steely eyes. It's as though she'd been holding them in reserve.

"Nobody's paying attention to what's actually happening out there. There's just no concept of how bad it really is. . . .

"I look at some of these juries—I can see it on their faces— they don't give a shit. Unless I can [argue] some sort of brain damage or something, they don't want to know a thing I'm saying. It's like, 'So what? What's the point? Why is she telling us all this stuff?'

"They don't want to know what's really going on in these kids' lives—the *real* reasons they do the things they do. They'd just as soon send them to the chair.

"People's consciousness has be raised. They have to start *listening,* start paying attention for a change. Human life has to matter more. *Kids* have to matter more. People have to learn again to care. . . .

"I don't know how we're going to do it—but that's our only hope."

23

"He should be in the electric chair. He shouldn't have the right to live. . . .

"I can see now—I never could before—why a person would want to own a gun. . . .

"I've lost my capacity for compassion. . . ."

Jackie Prince sits across from me, over a lunchtime salad in a Washington restaurant a block from her office at the Environmental Defense Fund. It is early January 1993. Her brother has been dead nearly two years. Two months from now, almost to the day, Dunc Fleming will be acquitted of his murder.

She is thirty, dark and pretty and very, very smart. An idealist-liberal. An activist with an engineering degree, who has made a career out of cleaning up the land. It's a safe bet she voted for Clinton. She's always opposed the death penalty. She loathes nothing more than the NRA.

And yet . . .

"I'm just so confused, so divided. I can't even articulate it. . . ."

Her fingers pull absently at the collar of a white turtleneck, then fall to the table and begin a rearrangement of the silverware. Her blue eyes well with tears, which she blinks back, attempting a smile. But it is a poor effort, and she knows it. After a moment, she gives up and wipes them dry.

Her voice is almost a whisper—as though if it weren't, it would be a scream.

"*HOW?* How can someone pull the trigger on a gun, and not think, 'I might *kill* this person'? How can there be no sense of that?

"If he was that incapable of feeling, of feeling anything at all—well then, he probably shouldn't even be here, he shouldn't be alive. . . .

"I get so sick of all this talk of victims. A beggar is a victim —not him. He's a *murderer.* He murdered my brother. He pulled that trigger. He'll do it again if he gets the chance. He'd be better off *dead.* . . ."

Jackie Prince, before her brother's death, lived for years in the city: New Haven, Connecticut, then Washington, D.C. Today, she says, she's afraid to be alone in her fiancé's South Boston apartment. She's even more afraid of the streets:

"I just want to live somewhere totally safe, where I don't have to be afraid to walk outside alone at night. I'm not proud of that—I can't help it. I just want to be safe. . . ."

And so, instead of Boston, Christian's sister says, she and her new husband will be looking for a place in the suburbs, where all the faces will be white.

Epilogue

Late March, 1994. I have not seen Dunc in more than a year. He's been transferred since then: to the New Haven Correctional Center on Whalley Avenue, where he is now nearly three years into his nine-year sentence on the conspiracy charge. He'll be out, he figures, in another eighteen months. That might be a fair guess ordinarily, though in Dunc's case there are other things to weigh.

It's been a very bad year. He appealed his conviction, and was released on an appeal bond last spring—after his sister Tanya raised $5,600 (most of it in twenty-dollar bills) on the street in a single afternoon. ("More money," she says today, "than I've ever seen in my life.") But there was an incident two months later, and he was back in jail that same night—this time on charges of threatening an officer and disturbing the peace.

"Bullshit" is what he calls it. "They was out there [on the street] takin' pictures, violatin' everybody's rights, trying to get some drug stuff goin' down. I told 'em to clear out, told 'em to take their stuff and go. . . .

"They shoved me in the cruiser. The cop that was there, he threw the first punch. Then they spray this can of mace in my face. . . ."

He was back on the street by late summer. Three days after Labor Day, he was busted and jailed again, this time for armed robbery:

"Me and this kid had a argument. He got robbed. Next thing I know, they hit me with a warrant. But it wasn't like what they said. I was just standin' next to this nigger, is all. . . ."

He's been in jail ever since. The ruling on his appeal has been postponed three times; it's scheduled now for late May. Sometime after that, probably by the fall, he'll be tried on the armed robbery charge—for which, if convicted, he could serve as much as twenty years. However things develop, it's not likely he'll be going anywhere soon.

He'll be twenty this fall. Thinner now, and duller-eyed, his walk more a shuffle than before. He is an hour late for our meeting, and seems barely to know he is there. He sits across from me, as listless as if drugged, in a windowless, beige-painted cinderblock holding cell in the basement of the Whalley Avenue jail. We are alone, the first time ever. Also for the first time, he no longer seems a boy. It is not hard at all, my face three feet from his, to see him as a middle-aged man.

He hasn't seen his parents in seven months—since the day he went back to jail last fall. His mother, he says, "comes all apart when she sees me in here. She be cryin' all the time like a kid." His father, he guesses, is just too sick to make the trip.

He has stopped taking classes. He no longer sees much point. He tried once last year, he tells me, during the time he was out on bail, to get Hillhouse High to re-admit him, "but they wouldn't take me back," he says. It's hard to know if I believe him, or—if I do—to know how hard he tried.

I ask what he thinks of when he thinks of Christian Prince:

"Changed my life, man, changed my life to stay. . . . Ever since then, I be out on the street, [the police], they be fuckin' with me everyday—don't *ever* be able to get no peace no more."

He doesn't want to talk about the future. "Hard to plan" is all he says, and shrugs. And when I bring up the street, and his "brothers," he mentions only one:

"My man Troy, they found him about ten days ago on this exit ramp somewhere. He had a bullet in his head."

He seems sadder now. Less cocky, more beaten. Even his smile seems sad. There is no talk now of malls or beaches, no brags about sex or guns. I tell him I'm on my way to see his family—he only nods and looks down. I remind him of his vow that his home will always be the 'Ville. He shrugs, then shakes his head:

"Maybe not. Maybe I leave . . . Most likely I be leavin'. I got no chance no more in this town. . . ."

A guard knocks now on our open door. Visitors' hours are over. I rise and shake his hand. It is as limp as dough. I wish him well—promise to send a copy of the book, make a small joke about the pictures they plan inside.

He seems not to hear, or care. He is standing now: his shoulders slumped, his chin almost on his chest. Then he raises it, and looks at me—it might be the first time he has met my eyes:

"I be seein' you again?" he asks. It is plain the answer he wants.

I'll stop by sometime, I tell him. I can't bring myself to speak the truth.

Jim and Julia Fleming haven't made it south yet—though Jim still swears they will. Julia, from all I can tell, doesn't care much either way. "It depends on the lottery," she says. She buys five tickets a week, and keeps hoping.

It's been an up-and-down year. A second child, Aaron, was born to Sandra last May. The Fleming girls have two apiece now; the household has swelled to eight. There are still no fathers of record, though the welfare payments took a jump.

Jim's left kidney gave out in November. "His whole body swole up," his wife says today. "Musta been a hundred pounds of fluid in there." He was in the hospital six weeks, and will begin dialysis in May.

Julia passed out in the kitchen on New Year's day—"My blood pressure just got too high, was all." She was in the hospital a week: "Some kinda heart problem. They never told me what."

Their twenty-fifth anniversary is coming up in June. I ask if they'll still be renewing their vows. "Guess we kinda forgot about that," Julia says.

Not much has changed in Newhallville, to judge by driving around. There are still packs of school-age kids, on weekday afternoons, at most corners on Dixwell and Shelton. The action is still heaviest after dark; the Oasis has reopened, though it is a juice bar today.

But those who live there feel a change:

"The shootings are down, way down," says Dunc's sister Sandra. "There's still as much dealin', but you don't hear the shots so much no more."

The numbers bear her out. There were twenty murders in New Haven in 1993, down from the high of thirty-four. And while it's still too soon to say that the corner has been turned (the nine homocides through the first three months of this year, with the warm weather still to come, don't bode well for the trend), it's clear at least that the problem is being faced.

There's a new approach in the city. "Community-based policing"—the dispersal of "substations" in high-crime neighborhoods all over town. There's been one in Newhallville now for close to two years.

It's a primitive notion, really—the friendly beat-cop always close at hand. But it comes with a high-tech twist: the Child Development–Community Policing Program, a marriage of Chief Nick Pastore's four-hundred-man department with the Child Study Center at Yale.

The idea is prevention. Street cops are trained in ghetto-child psychology by Yale's CSC staffers, linked with a network of support groups citywide, then assigned to the meanest streets.

"The hardest thing any cop has to deal with is a group of teenagers standing on a corner," one twenty-one-year veteran told a senior editor of *Yale Alumni Magazine*. "Understanding their mind-set is worth its weight in gold."

A simpler factor may be fear. Within the last year or so, says District Attorney Mike Dearington (who confesses that Dunc's murder acquittal "still nags at me a bit"), a joint state-federal task force has taken aim at gangs:

"We're trying them now in federal courts. These guys don't like that—they don't mind so much going to [Whalley Avenue], but you threaten them with a federal pen, it's going to make them think twice. . . .

"The Jungle Boys, the 'Ville, the Island Brothers—we've got most of their guys in jail. They're disassembled. Their leadership is gone."

Not everyone sees it that way. "It's just quiet now, is all," Sandra Fleming says. "It's always quiet this time of year. The dealers, they go to jail in winter, they're back on the street by June. Can't blame 'em, can you? It's cold out there right now. . . ."

Jackie Prince was married last June: to a man who arrived in her life the month before her brother left it. The two never met each other, though—in Christian's last phone call to his sister, the week before he died, her future husband was the biggest news.

On the program for the wedding service, whose guest list (on the Prince side) was drawn heavily from among those who'd been there for Christian's funeral, was this passage from Thorton Wilder:

> *Even memory is not necessary for love.*
> *There is a land of the dead,*
> *And a land of the living,*
> *And the bridge is love . . .*

Christian's sister, who once swore to me, still poisoned by her brother's death, that she was too afraid ever to live in the

city again, lives in the city today: in Cambridge, Massachu-
setts, in a condo, four blocks from Harvard Square.

"We are healing," she tells me now, sixteen months later
over the phone. "I have a new husband, a new beginning. New
beginnings help. But I think of him every day. . . ."

Sally Prince is better: "Less angry at least. I'm learning, I
guess, to live with the grief. But my faith in humanity, in
human goodness—that's gone forever, I'm afraid. I can't feel
the same about people anymore."

We talk by phone three days after Easter. There are fresh
flowers, she tells me, on Christian's grave this week.

Ted Prince still follows Yale lacrosse—"Every Monday morning I get the Baltimore paper, the only one with the scores. I've
got the team schedule in my pocket right now."

His son's old defense stick, the same one Ted carried with
him all afternoon on that day three years ago, still stands in its
place outside the living room door.

The memorial reading room at Lawrenceville hasn't happened yet—though the funds are still being raised. But something else has: The first recipient of the Christian Prince
Memorial Lacrosse Scholarship, a freshman named Brendan
Doyle, entered Yale University on a scholarship last fall.

The Brady Bill was passed last November, and took effect,
in most states, eleven days after the third anniversary of Christian's death.

There have been, so far, no more killings at Yale.